D1101494

NEEDLEPOINT

LETTS CREATIVE NEEDLECRAFTS

·SANDRA · HARDY·

LETTS CREATIVE NEEDLECRAFTS

NEEDLEPOINT

SANDRA HARDY

CHARLES LETTS · Letts of London® FOUNDED 1796

First published in 1992
by Charles Letts & Company Ltd
Letts of London House
Parkgate Road
London SW11 4NQ

Reprinted 1993

Designed and produced by Rosemary Wilkinson
4 Lonsdale Square, London N1 1EN

Editor: Hilary More
Illustrators: Mike Spiller, Mary Tomlin
Designer: Patrick Knowles
Photographer: Mark Gatehouse

© Charles Letts & Company Ltd 1992

All our Rights Reserved. No part of this publication may be
reproduced, stored in a retrieval system, or transmitted, in any form
or by any means, electronic, mechanical, photocopying, recording or
otherwise, without the prior permission of Charles Letts Publishers.

'Letts' is a registered trademark of Charles Letts & Company Ltd

A CIP catalogue record for this book is available from the British
Library

ISBN 1 85238 343 7

Typeset by Fakenham Photosetting Ltd, Fakenham, Norfolk

Printed in Belgium

CONTENTS

An 18th century chair cover with central figures worked in petit point and background in gros point.

DESIGN: PAST AND PRESENT

Needlepoint to many readers may also be known as canvaswork or tapestry, and there always seems to have been confusion about these terms. Needlepoint is the true name for embroidery worked over a canvas base, while tapestry is a woven fabric and canvaswork could strictly speaking include other crafts involving canvas.

Needlepoint as we know it today really started in the 16th century, with the English middle classes imitating the huge tapestries found in the aristocratic houses. Large wall hangings, bed curtains, carpets and cushion covers were worked in tent stitch on a linen canvas of 16–20 holes per 2.5 cm (1 in). Designs were often inspired by illustrations from printed books, or had floral, animal or insect motifs, prompted by the general enthusiasm for natural history. Individual motifs were often worked on canvas and then applied to a background fabric, as in the Oxburgh Hangings for example. These were worked by Mary Queen of Scots and Bess of Hardwick in 1567 in cross stitch using silk on a linen canvas.

Another special type of canvaswork was Turkey work, which was an attempt to imitate woven carpets. It was worked in coarse wool on linen canvas with rows of Turkey rug knots and was used for cushions, bench covers, chair seats and foot carpets. Also very popular in the latter part of the century were the vertical zigzag patterns using an Irish stitch, now known as Florentine or Bargello.

Smaller items of needlepoint became popular in the 17th century, when jewel boxes, caskets, mirror surrounds and samplers using a variety of stitches were stitched in silk. Designs were based on Bible stories or classical mythology and little care was taken to achieve correct sizes or proportions. Cushions were still used to soften stone ledges and wooden benches. They were worked in cross stitch and long-legged cross stitch in wool with silk highlights.

Dutch painters became a popular design source in the William & Mary period, leading to coarser canvases which would accommodate the bolder designs often of large flowers and leaves. As the century progressed there was increased demand for needlepoint chair coverings, stools, sofas and screens. These were mostly worked in wool in tent stitch on a 16 or 18 hole canvas and sometimes with petit point centre panels. From their European base the early settlers in North America took the needlepoint designs with them and while in the beginning there was little time for embroidery, as they became settled needlepoint gained in popularity and mirrored the advances in Europe.

The popularity of needlepoint continued into the 18th century, with settees and sets of matching chairs being covered. So important was the needlepoint that chairs were altered in size or even made to fit the covers. In addition needlepoint was used for folding card table tops, firescreens, pincushions, pole screens, candle sconces and kneelers. The love of floral patterns blossomed on both sides of the Atlantic, again with pastoral scenes often surrounded by floral borders. One well known set was the Boston Common series of fishing ladies, the designs for which came from contemporary engravings. Tent stitch continued to dominate, often with cross stitch borders for extra strength; however Florentine stitch often worked in silk increased in popularity. As the famous furniture designers, Chippendale, Adam, Kent, Sheraton and Hepplewhite emerged so the traditional needlepoint decorative designs and colourings gave way to the fashionable brocades, damasks and silk fabrics.

The early years of the 19th century saw a new type of needlepoint being introduced, Berlin woolwork. This originated in Germany and used a new type of wool, Zephyr, dyed with the new chemical dyes to produce bright and often crude colours, such as emerald green, crimson, magenta and yellow. Patterns were printed on squared paper, initially in black and white, but later in colour – the first charted designs. Berlin canvas was also

supplied initially made of silk and dyed in pastel colours which was sufficiently attractive for small areas to be left unstitched.

The popularity of the Berlin woolwork continued to increase both in Europe and America and extended from upholstery, cushions, carpets, firescreens and table tops to slippers, waistcoats, pincushions and door plates.

Penelope (double) canvas was invented in the 1830s and was stronger and easier to work with than the earlier silk canvas. It soon became the more popular and had the added advantage that gros and petit point could be worked together. Designs of this period were classical, geometric and historical as well as depicting animals and birds, but most of all they were floral, especially featuring cabbage roses. Backgrounds were worked in solid colours such as dark red, blue or black. Cross stitch predominated with some Victorian tufting known today as pile or plush stitch, also canvas lace, crochet and bead work were included.

Towards the end of the century there was much condemnation of the brilliant colours and lack of original design used in Berlin woolwork. Its popularity began to decline accelerated by the Japanese-inspired Aesthetic Movement, which demanded pale, subtle colours and oriental designs. Also the overstuffed Victorian furniture was popular and this was unsuitable for needlepoint covers. The decline was pushed further by William Morris and the Arts and Crafts Societies with their demands for individual hand-crafted articles, together with a return to the old dyestuffs and colours. The Royal School of Needlework was formed in London 1872 with the aim of improving design and technique but unfortunately needlepoint was thought to be too restrictive and consequently ignored.

A few key embroiderers bridged the years to the present century, for example Louisa Pesel, the first president of the Embroiderers' Guild, who was commissioned by the Dean of Westminster to produce kneelers, long cushions and alms bags in needlepoint. After the wars the popularity of needlepoint kneelers increased and in many churches today there are sets of kneelers worked by local embroidery groups.

Between the two World Wars, much thought was given to the design of all embroidery and many Bauhaus and Modern Movement ideas succeeded in freeing needlepoint from the restrictive rules of the Victorian era. Exciting and abstract designs were produced, for example Duncan Grant's Prie Dieu chair covering, produced by the Omega Workshop.

Following a fairly static period after the Second World War there was renewed interest in needlepoint which has continued until the present day. A great deal of hard work has been done by the art schools showing students how to develop their own designs and likewise by the Embroiderers' Guild and the Royal School of Needlework who have helped by promoting different exhibitions. Needlepoint kits, magazines and books are in abundance with a vast array of designs and techniques being shown. The Embroiderers' Guild continues to promote an experimental approach to needlepoint, encouraging original ideas using unusual threads and materials. There is now more leisure time available and individual, hand-crafted items are again much valued.

The projects in this book cover a wide range of stitches and are designed to be of use in the home. There are also many more ideas for experimental work as an extension of the techniques presented.

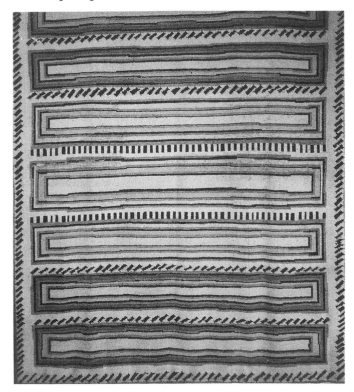

A graphic tapestry designed by Duncan Grant for the Omega workshops, c. 1914.

The projects in this book employ a variety of stitches, threads and canvas, starting with a simple needlecase and progressing to the more demanding, but equally enjoyable firescreen.

CANVAS

Needlepoint canvas is a fairly stiff, open weave material with evenly-spaced threads. Canvas is usually made of stiffened cotton, although linen and silk are available.

The size of the canvas is measured by its mesh count, that is the number of holes to 2.5cm (1 in). The higher the number the finer the canvas. The mesh size will affect the pattern, with a high count you can work a very detailed design, but it will take longer to complete the project. The smaller, closely-worked stitches will also be more durable.

The two main variations of canvas weave are single and double. The single or mono canvas is made up of interwoven horizontal and vertical threads. An improved version is interlocked canvas, where each vertical thread is made up of two thinner threads and woven around the horizontal thread, making a much more stable mesh. Single canvas sizes range from $3\frac{1}{3}$ for an open-mesh rug canvas to 30 per 2.5 cm (1 in) for the finest work. The usual canvas for cushions and chair seats is 10, 12 or 14 holes per 2.5 cm (1 in).

Double or Penelope canvas has interwoven pairs of horizontal and vertical threads. As there are double the number of threads to the 2.5 cm (1 in), there are double the number of holes, so this canvas can be used for really fine work. Double canvas is often worked in petit point, which is invaluable for stitching areas of fine detail. Penelope or double canvas is also measured by holes per 2.5 cm (1 in) but the threads are sometimes counted as well, for example 14/28 means 14 holes and 28 threads.

Canvas is generally white or antique brown in colour. Choose the colour that is the nearest shade to the threads used in the project. If the canvas is not being completely covered, it can easily be painted as described in the Skill File on page 16. Widths of canvas vary from 46 to 120 cm (18 to 48 in). Choose whichever is the most economical for the project, remembering that needlepoint can be worked in any direction on a piece of canvas.

The quality of canvas is indicated by the price. For projects expected to withstand hard wear use the best quality for strength and durability. This has a more polished and smoother finish than the cheaper versions and does not have the flaws or uneven threads, which can cause distorted stitching. When buying canvas for a project allow an extra 7.5 cm (3 in) all round to allow for stretching and mounting when the embroidery is finished.

Plastic canvas is a relative newcomer to needlepoint and as well as being perfect for 3D articles, for example, boxes, napkin rings and decorations, it is also a useful canvas for beginners and children. Normally transparent in colour, plastic canvas is sold in small sheets or pre-cut shapes such as circles or ovals with 5, 7 or 10 holes to 2.5 cm (1 in). Plastic canvas can be cut into any shape without fraying.

THREADS

The most widely-used threads for needlepoint are tapestry, crewel and Persian wools. For articles needing to withstand wear and tear these natural yarns must be used. However for more decorative items, other yarns or threads can be used or introduced as a highlight, for example, knitting wool, fine ribbon, thin strips of fabric and embroidery threads.

Always buy sufficient yarn to finish the project at the beginning, as shades may vary from batch to batch.

Tapestry Wool
A tightly twisted 4-ply wool suitable for 10 or 12 hole canvas. Tapestry wool can be used double on coarser canvas or on a finer canvas when straight stitched. Tapestry wool is available in 10m (11 yd) skeins or 20 g hanks.

Crewel Wool
A fine 2-ply single strand wool, slightly finer than Persian wool. Three strands of crewel wool are needed to cover a 12 or 14 hole canvas. The great advantage crewel wool has over tapestry wool is the

opportunity it provides for combining different shades in the needle to create subtle blending. Crewel wool can be bought in 25m (27¼ yd) skeins or 50 g hanks.

Persian Wool

A loosely-twisted 2-ply stranded wool, slightly thicker than crewel wool, the strands can also be separated and blended together in the same way. The equivalent thicknessess are two strands of Persian wool equals three strands of crewel wool or one strand of tapestry wool. This wool is available in 7.3m (8 yd) skeins.

Stranded Cotton

A semi-shiny 6-strand thread that is easily separated and blended together. Stranded cotton is available in a huge range of colours in 8m (8¾ yd) skeins. Six strands will fill a 14 hole canvas.

Stranded Silk

Available as a twisted thread rather than stranded and in a four to seven stranded thread which can be easily divided. This thread is expensive compared to stranded cotton and available in 5 m (5½ yd) skeins. Silk tends to catch more and so is not such an easy thread to stitch, but it does create a beautiful sheen to the finished piece.

Soft Embroidery Cotton

A single strand 5-ply cotton thread, that is soft to work with and produces a flat matt finish. This cotton is available in 10m (11 yd) skeins.

Perlé Cotton

A twisted 2-ply thread, producing a shiny finish. It is available in 22m (24½ yd) skeins.

Rug Yarn

This wool has a tough, coarse texture and varies from 2 to 8 ply. A 6-ply rug wool would be used for a 5 hole canvas. Thrums are a good, cheap alternative, available in 2-ply, they are the threads left-over from carpet weaving looms.

Needles

Tapestry needles have large eyes to enable easy threading and blunt ends so they can pass easily through the canvas without splitting either the canvas thread or the yarn when working into a hole already containing one thread. Sizes range from 13 (the largest) to 26 (the smallest). For a 10 hole canvas use size 18, for a 12/14 hole canvas use a size 20 and for a 16/18 hole canvas use a size 22. Make sure that the needle eye is large enough to take the chosen yarn without fraying and, once threaded, can pass through the canvas without forcing the threads apart and distorting the weave.

Frames

If using a frame (see page 17), choose from a stretcher, rotating or slate frame, which can be hand-held or floor-standing for larger items.

A stretcher frame is a basic frame similar to a picture frame. The pairs of stretchers slot together to produce a working area that should be slightly larger than the canvas.

Rotating frames are made of two rollers on which a strip of cotton webbing is stapled. The top and base edges of the canvas are stitched to the webbing. These frames are made in several sizes.

Slate frames are similar to rotating frames, but more sturdily constructed. Slate frames are also available in a variety of sizes as well as with a floor stand.

Embroidery hoops can be used for canvaswork, but only for very small pieces using very fine canvas. Bind round the outer ring of the hoop with cotton tape before fitting in the canvas, otherwise the ring will mark the canvas.

The latest addition to the range are PVC tubular clip-on frames.

Other Equipment

One important piece of equipment is a good pair of small sharp embroidery scissors. You will also need masking tape, needle and thread for attaching the canvas to the frame, and drawing pins, board, set square and a fine water spray for blocking. Also available are a range of magnifiers which can prove very helpful for reading charts and checking yarn colours.

Adequate lighting is important, especially when choosing yarns. For evening stitching, daylight simulation bulbs can be very effective. Make sure you are sitting in a comfortable chair with a good back support.

PREPARING AND STARTING TO SEW

Preparing the Canvas

Canvas should always be cut along a thread in both directions. Remember to allow at least 7.5 cm (3 in) extra all the way around, unless the project is very small when 5 cm (2 in) will be sufficient.

Before you begin, enclose all the raw edges of the canvas with strips of masking tape (diagram 1). This will prevent the canvas from

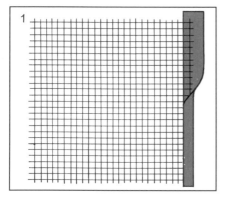

fraying. Fold the masking tape evenly in half over the raw edges and press firmly in place. Alternatively, a cotton tape can be hand-stitched over the edges in the same way.

If the project needs to be blocked and stretched back into shape when completed (see page 73), then it is important to make an outline shape of the finished piece on a sheet of paper. This can be worked out from the charts. If you are in any doubt that the chosen yarns will not completely cover the canvas, then it is best to paint it. Either use watered-down acrylic paints, spray

paints or fabric paints. Alternatively, work a small test piece using the yarn and the canvas and working in the main stitch. If you are not happy with the coverage, alter the thread amount or change the mesh size of the canvas.

Lastly, the centre of the canvas should be marked to match up with the centre point of the chart. There are two ways to do this. For the first use a permanent pen to mark the canvas. Test the pen in water before you begin, to check that it is waterproof, if not, when the needlepoint is stretched at the end of the stitching the pen dye can ruin the piece. Fold the canvas in half both ways following a line of canvas; unfold and mark along both lines with the pen. You may also find it helpful to mark a grid on the canvas to match up with the working chart (diagram 2).

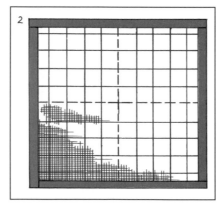

For the second method, use a tape measure to find the centre, then mark vertically and horizontally with a line of basting stitches. For

some designs it may be a good idea to mark the top of the canvas.

Working from a Chart

All the projects in this book are stitched from charts. Remember that each square on the chart represents one stitch and these must be counted as threads on the canvas.

If you lose your place on the chart whilst working, try colouring in the squares as you stitch. Or, use one of the weighted magnifiers, which will help to keep your place as well as enlarging the symbols.

Threads and Quantities

When working needlepoint use a thread approximately 46 cm (18 in) long. Too long and the thread will tangle and become worn where it is held in the needle. As you stitch, move the needle along the yarn often to avoid weakening the yarn at the point of the eye. If the yarn keeps tangling and knotting while you work, you are probably working in the wrong direction. Run your fingers along the length of yarn, one direction will seem smoother, like the pile of a fabric. Always cut the yarn with scissors, if you break the thread it will become weak and stretched.

Tapestry needles have large eyes and are therefore easy to thread. However, if you have a problem, either use a purchased needle threader or use the following method. Wrap the thread around the needle and hold it tightly. Slide the thread off the end of the needle and still holding it tightly, push it through the eye of the needle.

The quantities are given for each project; you will need one skein of each shade unless otherwise stated.

Stitching

Try to work with an even tension, that is the amount the stitches are pulled across the canvas threads. Working in a frame will help you achieve a good stitch rhythm. Always complete a row rather than stopping in the middle, as this can cause a ridge in the finished surface.

Never use unpicked wool as it will be thinner and will not cover the canvas properly.

Do not jump from one area to another of the same colour, but finish off and start again.

Never let loose ends dangle on the wrong side or they can become caught up in the stitching and be pulled through to the right side.

Wherever possible bring the needle up in an empty hole and take it down into a partially filled one to help to smooth down the yarn.

After several stitches the thread may become twisted, resolve this by letting the needle and thread dangle down to untwist themselves.

There are no hard and fast rules about the order of stitching a design, however if you begin at the top and work downwards you will not disturb the stitched area. Work any border first, as it will hold the

canvas firm while the centre is being worked. Work any dark colours before pale colours, so they do not become discoloured.

Using a Frame

It is often a matter of personal preference whether to use a frame of not. When the stitches lie horizontally or vertically on the wrong side as with cross stitch or basketweave stitch, then a frame is not essential. However, if the stitches lie diagonally, the canvas will be pulled in one direction causing distortion. This is easily prevented by using a frame.

Rotating or slate frames are the most suitable frames for the projects in this book. The frame must be wide enough for the required canvas width, any excess length can be wound round one of the horizontal rollers.

To fit a canvas in a frame, first turn under 2.5 cm (1 in) at top and bottom of canvas and back stitch to the tape fixed to the rollers of the frame, using a double sewing or button thread (diagram 3). Make sure that the sides of the canvas are parallel to the sides of the frame. Adjust the tension, using the nuts or screws until the canvas is taut. Thread a large needle with button thread and lace the sides of the canvas to the sides of the frame (diagram 4). If the canvas is large, these side lacings will have to be undone and replaced as the canvas is wound round the rollers.

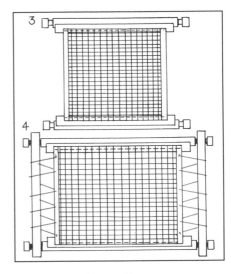

Starting and Finishing

Start with a knot on the right side of the canvas, approximately 2.5 cm (1 in) away from where you want to stitch and in the direction that you will be stitching towards (diagram 5). When the thread on the wrong side has been stitched over several times, snip off the knot. When finishing a length of yarn, run the needle under several stitches on the wrong side, then snip off the end of the thread (diagram 6).

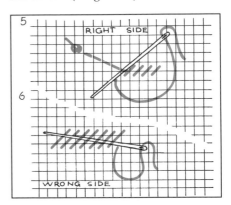

TARTAN NEEDLECASE

Worked in simple cross stitch this smart tartan needlecase is the perfect project for a beginner. The six shades of blue and green are highlighted with a dash of scarlet.

Quick and easy to stitch, this needlecase is worked on a relatively large 10 hole canvas. The colours are typically tartan, but can be changed to match a well-loved work box or basket. As the case only uses small amounts of yarn it is a good way of using up oddments left over from larger projects. The simple check design can be easily repeated to use on larger items. When the chart is stitched twice it produces a 18 cm (7 in) square and this could be used as the centre of a cushion. Work the chart eight times for a complete cover, a chair seat or an attractive screen. In the same way, by working only half the chart you would create an attractive pincushion to match the needlecase.

Cord, see page 56

REQUIREMENTS		
1 piece of antique interlock canvas with 10 holes per 2.5 cm (1 in), 25 × 16.5 cm (10 × 6½ in)		
Tapestry needle size 18		
Masking tape		
1 piece of lightweight wadding 18 × 9 cm (7 × 3½ in)		
1 piece of blue felt 15 × 8 cm (6 × 3 in)		
Matching sewing thread		
Clear fabric adhesive		
Stranded cotton in red		
Small curved needle		

Cord, see page 56
Tapestry wool as follows:

Colour	Appletons	Anchor
Cornflower	463	8688
Scarlet	503	8204
Leaf Green	428	8992
Cornflower	462	8686
Bright china blue	747	8632
Peacock blue	647	8884

Finished size
18 × 9 cm (7 × 3½ in)

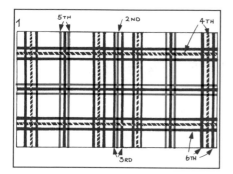

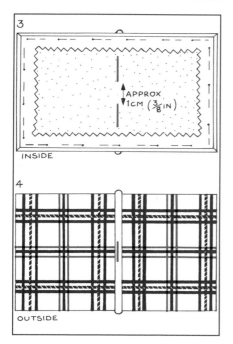

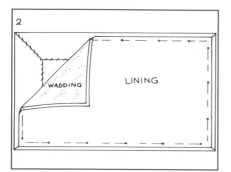

PREPARATION

Bind over the raw edges of the canvas and mark the centre as described in the Skill File (page 16). You will not need a frame when working this design. Trim round the piece of felt with pinking shears.

STITCHING

Work the design (opposite) throughout in cross stitch (page 32) using 1 strand of tapestry wool.

Stitch the medium blue edges first, then the red spine and the medium blue centre lines and either side of red spine. Stitch the green stripes, red stripes and lastly the pale blue stripes (diagram 1).

MAKING UP

When the stitching is complete, trim the canvas to within 1.5cm (⅝ in) of the worked area. Press on the wrong side over a damp cloth, then press in the edges, so that the second row of blue stitching lies on the wrong side. Mitre the corners of canvas, as described in the Skill File (page 72). Slipstitch the edge of canvas to the wrong side of the needlepoint (diagram 2).

Stick the wadding to the wrong side of the needlepoint, trimming if necessary to fit. Place the lining fabric centrally over the wadding; fold under raw edges and pin in place so that the unstitched canvas is hidden. Position the felt in the centre of the lined case and attach through all layers by two long

stitches, worked in embroidery cotton, securing the centre of the cord on the outside of the case at the same time (diagram 3). Begin and end the embroidery thread between the lining and the canvas. Secure the ends of the cord onto the canvas hem; trim and cover with the lining. Slipstitch the lining to the canvas all round.

EXPERIMENTING

This tartan design is ideal for changing the colours to your own favourites. The sample on page 18 shows how a change of colour scheme can make the case look completely different. For this sample we used:

Colour	Appletons	Anchor
Fuchsia pink	801	8488
Leaf green	421	9112
Bright mauve	454	8526
Bright mauve	451	8522
Signal green	428	8992
Purple	104	8592

As tartans and checks are made up of straight lines it is very easy to chart your own tartan design or work another recognized one. The second chart shown here is of a familiar Scottish tartan – the Macleod. To make your own pattern chart use 10 lines per 2.5 cm (1 in) graph paper and coloured pencils. Draw in the outlines and centre lines. Mark in the other lines noting particularly which ones predominate over the others. Finally fill in background areas.

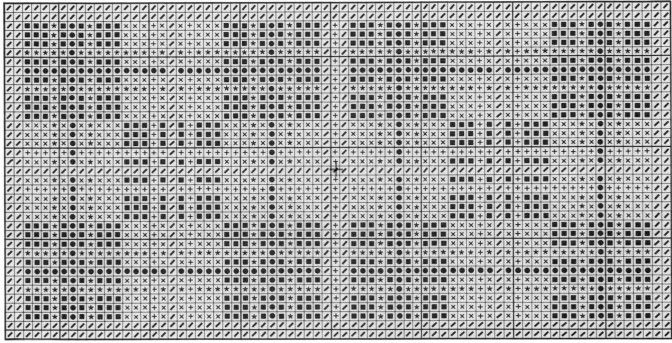

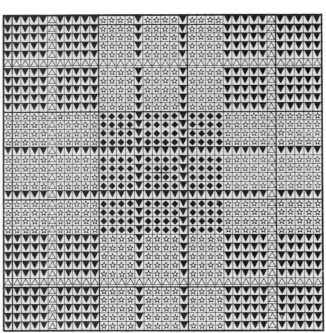

KEY ▲
- ✎ cornflower 463
- + scarlet 503
- ● leaf green 428
- ★ cornflower 462
- ■ bright china blue 747
- ✕ peacock blue 647

KEY ▶
- ▼ yellow
- △ pink
- ☆ grey
- ◆ black

FLOWER FRAME

Surround your favourite picture or photograph with a
delightful picture frame. The delicate pink-hued flowers are
worked in diagonal bands across
a pale turquoise background.

This repeating flower pattern has been worked
in four alternating quarters to create an
attractive diamond shape around the picture.
Decide where to position the finished frame
and match the colours to the surrounding
decor. The frame edges can be enlarged by
moving the four quarters outwards by an

equal amount, or reduced, to make up a set of
frames in different sizes and colours. The
frame can be free-standing or wall-hung.

The pattern could also be continued across
the central opening and the worked
needlepoint used to make an unusual cover for
a book or a decorative table mat.

REQUIREMENTS

1 piece of white interlock
canvas with 12 holes to
2.5 cm (1 in), 36 × 31cm
(14 × 12¼ in)
Tapestry needle size 20
Masking tape
Frame (optional)
1 piece of aqua-coloured
lining fabric 30 × 25cm
(12 × 10 in)
Matching sewing thread

2 pieces of mounting board
each 25 × 19.75 cm (9¾
× 7¾ in)
Clear fabric adhesive
Pins
Steel rule and set square
Craft knife and cutting board
Tapestry wool as follows:

Colour	Appletons	Anchor
Bright rose pink	946	8438
Bright rose pink	944	8416
Turquoise (× 2)	524	8916
Rose pink (1 hank)	751	8392

Finished size
25 × 20 cm (10 × 8 in)

PREPARATION

Bind the raw edges of the canvas and mark the centre as described in the Skill File (page 16). Draw lines vertically and horizontally through the centre to divide the canvas into four equal parts.

To mark the stitched frame areas, count 23 threads to the left and then to the right of the vertical centre line and mark a line on the next row of holes. Then count 36 threads above and below the horizontal centre line and mark. These will be the inside frame lines. For the outside frame lines, count 26 threads both vertically and horizontally from the inside ones and draw lines. To help position the flowers in the design, mark vertical and horizontal lines across the canvas every 10 lines to coincide with the chart lines. Use a waterproof marking pen in a different colour to distinguish them from the frame lines.

Mount the canvas into a frame as described in the Skill File (page 17).

STITCHING

Use one thread of tapestry wool throughout.

Begin by stitching the turquoise line at A and work to B (diagram 1) and then back to A using basketweave stitch (page 32). Stitch turquoise lines above and below this at the correct intervals until the first quarter is complete (see chart opposite). Repeat, to stitch the

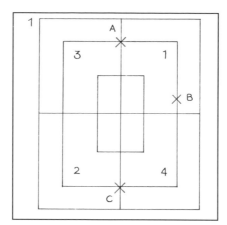

diagonally opposite quarter of the frame in the same way, starting at C. To stitch quarters 3 and 4 use backstitch (page 33) instead of basketweave stitch.

Begin stitching the flowers in medium pink, then dark pink and lastly work the turquoise stalks. Work the flowers in continental tent stitch (page 32). Place all the starting knots for the flowers 1.5 cm ($\frac{5}{8}$ in) below each flower to avoid the stitching. Remember to stitch the flowers in the opposite direction in sections 2 and 4.

Stitch in the background in basketweave stitch, taking care to interweave the pink threads through the turquoise lines and flower motifs. Finally the inside and outside turquoise lines can be stitched in half cross stitch (page 32).

MAKING UP AND FINISHING

Using the knife, rule, set square and cutting board, trim down one piece of mounting board, so that it is

slightly smaller on each side, for the frame back. Cut out the inside rectangle from larger mounting board, leaving a frame of 5 cm (2 in).

Trim the outside edges of the canvas to within 2.5cm (1 in) of the worked canvas and cut across the corners to within 1 cm ($\frac{3}{8}$ in) of the stitching. Cut out the excess canvas in the centre of the frame leaving 2.5 cm (1 in) border of unworked canvas. Snip into the corners up to the stitching (diagram 2). Dab a small

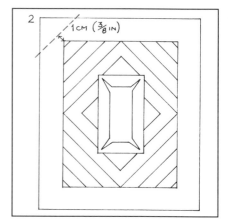

amount of adhesive underneath the corners to strengthen them.

Position the stitched canvas over the cardboard and pin to top and inside edges, making sure that the stitched lines are parallel to the card edges and that the canvas is firmly stretched (diagram 3). Lightly dab the wrong side of the card with adhesive and press down the canvas, mitring the corners (see page 72). Alternatively, use masking tape to stick the canvas onto the card.

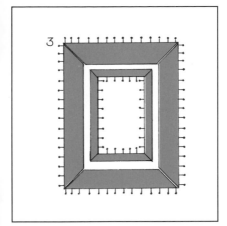

Cover the back card with lining fabric in the same way. Place the back to frame front, with wrong sides together, matching edges. Slipsitch around the outer edges, leaving one side open. Insert the picture and slipstitch to close.

To hang the frame, sew on 2 small rings at the back and attach a cord between them. For a free-standing frame, take a piece of card the same size as the back of the frame. Score

a horizontal line two-thirds of the way down and bend carefully. Glue the top third to the back of the frame.

At the bottom, attach a cord between card and back to keep the card in the desired position (diagram 4).

EXPERIMENTING

To change the look of the frame, use stranded cottons – this will give the frame a shiny effect. Use eight strands of embroidery cotton in the needle at all times, to cover the canvas.

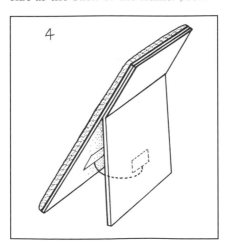

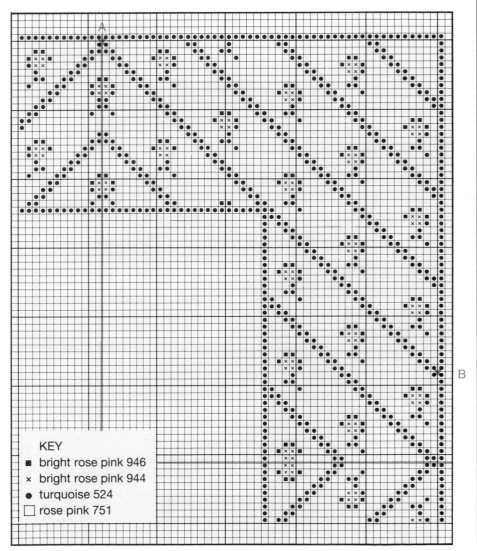

KEY
- ■ bright rose pink 946
- × bright rose pink 944
- ● turquoise 524
- □ rose pink 751

HI-TECH DOORSTOP

We used modern computer technology to create an abstract design for a doorstop. Wrap the canvas round a standard house brick to provide the traditional shape.

Using a home computer and a Paint software program, this design was quickly and easily developed. The computer mouse replaced the pencil for drawing the pattern onto the colour screen. The lines and shapes were moved about and re-coloured as the ideas flowed, until the design looked good. To prevent the curved shapes from becoming too angular or stepped, the design is worked over a 14 hole canvas. Tapestry wool is used for the coral squiggles and blue vermicelli, but crewel wool provides the flatter background. To help achieve the lines and irregular shapes the whole doorstop is worked in tent stitch.

REQUIREMENTS

1 piece of antique interlock canvas with 14 holes per 2.5 cm (1 in), 47 × 37 cm (18½ × 14½ in)
Tapestry needle size 22
Masking tape
Frame
House brick, 21.5 × 10 × 6 cm (8½ × 4 × 2½ in)
1 piece of curtain interlining 40 × 38 cm (16 × 15 in)

Matching sewing thread
Small curved needle
1 piece of black calico 23 × 12.5 cm (9 × 5 in)
Clear fabric adhesive
Tapestry wool as follows:

Colour	Appletons	Anchor
Coral	861	9532
Coral	862	8232
Cornflower (× 2)	463	8688
Crewel wool:	*Appletons*	*Paterna*
Bright china blue (1½ hanks)	747	500

Finished size
22 × 11 cm (8⅝ × 4¼ in)

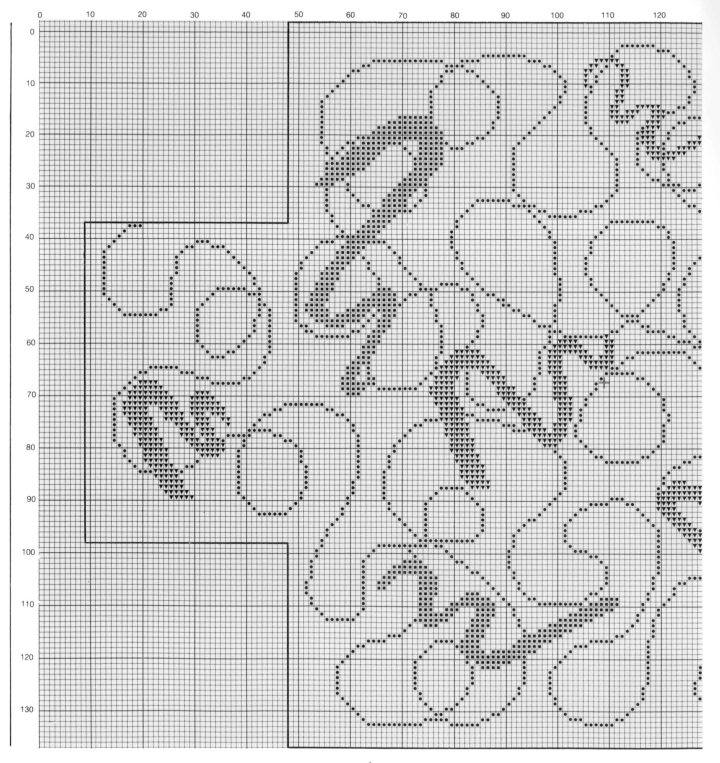

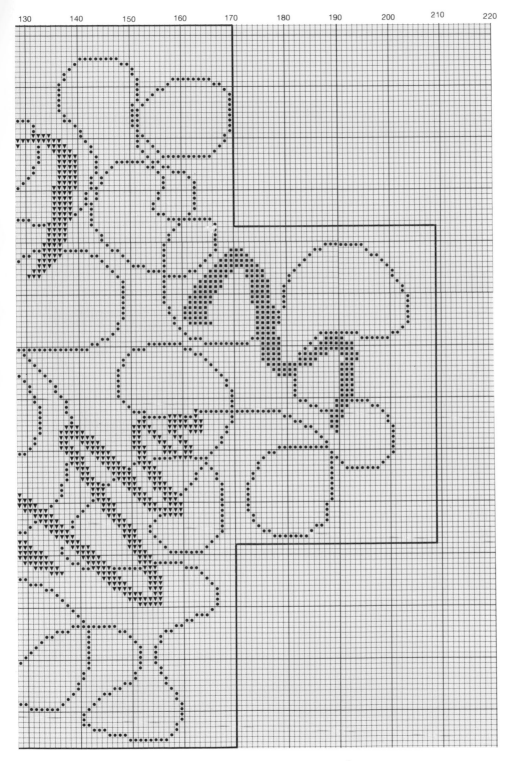

KEY
■ coral 861
▲ coral 862
● cornflower 463
□ bright china blue 747

PREPARATION

Bind over the canvas edges and mark the centre, as described in the Skill File (page 16). Measure out from the centre and mark the outline of the brick (diagram 1).

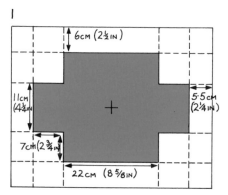

1

6cm (2½IN)

11cm (4¼IN)

5·5cm (2¼IN)

7cm (2¾IN)

22cm (8⅝IN)

Attach the canvas to the frame as described in the Skill File (page 17).

Measure and cut the interlining for padding the brick. Place the brick on the interlining at E (diagram 2) and fold up ends C and D. Fold A up one long side of the brick, enclosing the side edges of C and D. Pin to hold. Fold B over the top of the brick, then pin to A and to the

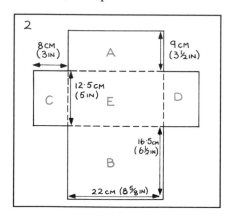

2

8cm (3IN)

A

9cm (3½IN)

12·5cm (5IN)

C

E

D

16·5cm (6½IN)

B

22cm (8⅝IN)

sides and top of C and D. Trim the edges of B, so that it lies flush with top edge of the brick. Finally herringbone stitch all edges using a curved needle and matching thread.

STITCHING

Use two strands of crewel wool and work throughout in tent stitch (page 32).

Following the chart on pages 28 and 29, stitch the coral areas first, then blue lines. Where the blue line crosses a stitched coral area, carefully thread the blue yarn through the back of the coral stitches on the wrong side of the canvas and proceed with the rest of the line. Stitch the background last.

Remove the canvas from the frame and check the fit over the padded brick, the stitched areas should just wrap underneath. You may need to add an extra couple of rows of stitching all the way around.

MAKING UP AND FINISHING

Cut out the four unwanted squares of canvas to within 1.5 cm (⅝ in) of

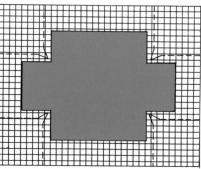

3

stitched area. Carefully snip into the corners up to the stitching (diagram 3). Dab a small amount of adhesive underneath the corners to strengthen them.

Place the wrapped brick on the wrong side of the canvas and fold the ends onto the underneath of the brick. Wrap the canvas turnings round the corners and lace the two ends together (diagram 4) as described in the Skill File (page 72).

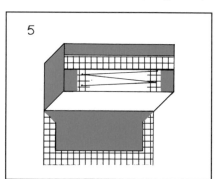

4

Fold in the sides in the same way, making sure that the unstitched edges of canvas on the sides are folded in. Lace these edges together and slipstitch up the side edges where the canvas meets (diagram 5).

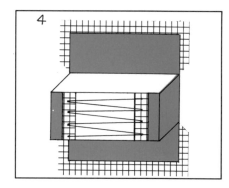

5

Place the black calico centrally over the base of the brick, turn in raw edges all round so they are 6 mm (¼ in) from outer edges and slipstitch to canvas.

Experimenting

Using a Paint program on the computer helps to create prototypes quickly and easily, moving from inspiration to design in minutes rather than the hours it takes to chart something on a grid paper. The computer's drawing device is called a mouse and you move this over the screen (the background) leaving blue lines in place. Next the orange squiggles are laid on top. The colour combinations can be tested by printing out the result on a colour printer (if available). Any part of the design can be moved to a different area, turned over, resized, scaled or rotated, helping to create many other intricate effects. The chosen design is then saved and filed on a computer disk and is easily retrieved as further ideas develop. Computer graphics makes the designing fun and offers the possibility to experiment with a limitless range of ideas. Finally the work can be printed out either as a template or in full colour as below, providing a valuable reference as the project is worked.

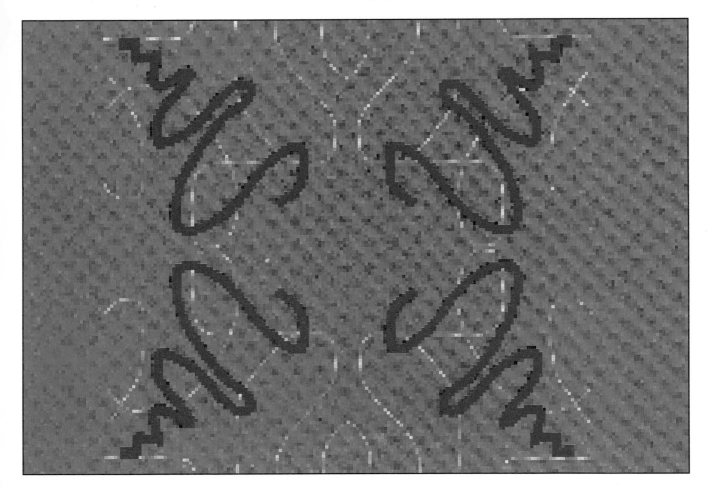

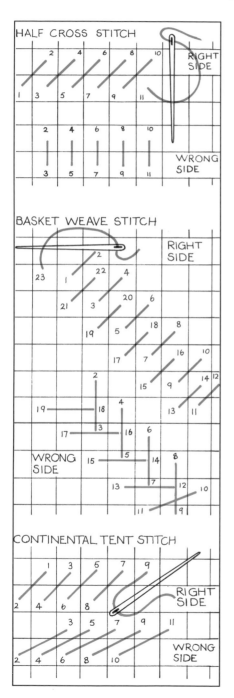

Half cross, basketweave and continental tent stitch all appear from the right side to be exactly the same. However, from the wrong side they are quite different, as are their uses and their effect on the canvas.

Half cross stitch

This is the quickest and easiest of the three stitches using the least amount of yarn. A disadvantage of this stitch, however, is that it does not always cover the canvas completely at the front and makes no attempt to do so at the back.

Work from left to right. If the rows are of reasonable length, then it is better to finish the yarn at the end of the row and start the next row on the left again. If the row is short, then work the row from right to left. At the end of the row, turn the canvas completely round and work the next row in the same direction.

Form each stitch by working diagonally over one canvas intersection, taking a straight stitch on the wrong side of the canvas.

Basketweave or diagonal tent stitch

This stitch is worked diagonally across the canvas and has the advantage of not distorting the canvas while covering the back of the piece, making it very suitable for hard wearing items. Check on the wrong side of the canvas, on one row the stitches lie vertically and on the next row they are horizontal, thus counteracting one

another. The disadvantage of this stitch is that it is difficult to work on small areas or in vertical or horizontal lines.

Work down the canvas with each stitch taken over one canvas intersection. The needle will be making vertical stitches on the wrong side. In the next row working up the canvas the needle is held horizontally.

Continental tent stitch

This is the most versatile of the stitches, but has the disadvantage of causing severe distortion to the canvas, unless it is well framed. Again the yarn is taken over one canvas intersection but longer diagonal stitches are formed on the wrong side, providing ample padding for hard wearing articles. As with half cross stitch, turn the canvas to work the return row.

Cross stitch

This was the most popular stitch used by the Victorians in England especially in their Berlin woolwork. This stitch has two advantages, firstly it does not cause any distortion to the canvas and secondly it pads the front of the canvas, making it hard wearing. Its disadvantages are that it is time consuming, uses a large amount of yarn and does not attempt to cover the reverse side of the canvas.

It can be worked from left to right for the first half cross and then from right to left crossing over these stitches or by completing each

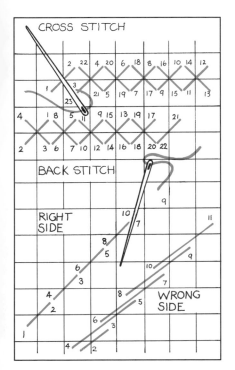

cross stitch before going on to the next stitch. Always make sure that the top halves of all the stitches lie in the same direction.

Back stitch

For thin lines of pattern or for outlining a design sometimes the only stitch to use is back stitch. However, it makes the wrong side of the canvas bulky as well as using large quantities of yarn.

To work back stitch horizontally, either stitch from left to right or right to left. Bring the needle out of one hole and take it back over 1 vertical canvas thread, bringing the needle out again two vertical canvas threads in front. This stitch can be

worked vertically and diagonally in the same way.

Choosing the Right Canvas

When experimenting you may have to decide what size canvas to use. It can be a matter of personal preference, but the design must be taken into account, too large a canvas might not give sufficient detail and any curved shapes will become too angular.

Always try out a small part of the design on a different canvas size to check how it looks. As a guide, to fill a 2.5 cm (1 in) square of canvas you will need 100 stitches on a 10 hole canvas, 144 stitches on a 12 hole canvas, 196 stitches on a 14 hole canvas and 256 stitches to fill a 16 hole canvas.

Transferring a Design

When you do not have a chart to follow, you will need to transfer the design onto the canvas. The easiest way to do this is to draw up the design to the finished size making sure that it has a solid black outline.

Place the clear drawing centrally under the canvas; check that the design is square on the canvas and hold firm with paper clips or masking tape. You should be able to see the outline clearly through the canvas mesh. Go over the design lines with a permanent waterproof pen (diagram 1). Remove the design and paint in the outlines in the chosen yarn colours. This method is not strictly accurate, so it is not suitable for a repeat pattern.

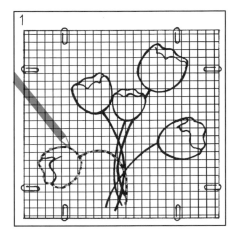

Estimating the Yarn

If you want to try some of the experimental ideas or your own needlepoint projects, you will need to know how to estimate the yarn amounts. These will depend on the size of canvas, the yarn used and the type of stitch. The best way is to work a test 2.5 cm (1 in) square and multiply the yarn as necessary. To give some idea of coverage, here are some examples showing the amount of yarn needed to cover a 2.5 cm (1 in) square for some of the most commonly-used stitches worked on different sizes of canvas.

Stitch	Yarn	Canvas	Quantity
Half Cross	Tapestry	10	70 cm (27½ in)
Tent	Tapestry	10	1m (1 yd)
Half Cross	Tapestry	12	80 cm (31½ in)
Tent	Tapestry	12	1.3m (1½ yd)
Cross	2 Crewel	14	2.3m (2½ yd)

ART DECO CUSHION PANEL

Combine the artistic talents of a well known 1920s potter with
a variety of textured stitches and create a highly-individual
cushion centre. Outline the needlework
with eyecatching piping.

One of the leading British art deco potters, Clarice Cliff, was the inspiration behind this fun pattern. The design, typical of the 1920s provides large areas of colour which have become the perfect backdrop for displaying a range of decorative needlepoint stitches. To add to the effect, certain areas have been highlighted with perlé cotton.

REQUIREMENTS

1 piece of interlock white
  canvas with 12 holes to
  2.5 cm (1 in), 49.5 × 23
  (19½ × 9 in)
Tapestry needle size 20
Masking tape
Frame
3 m (3⅓ yd) of piping cord
50 cm (½ yd) yellow chintz
  fabric
50 cm (⅝ yd) of 122 cm
  (48 in) wide pastel green
  chintz
Matching sewing thread

Cushion pad 39.5 cm
  (15½ in) square
2 skeins of DMC cotton
  perlé 746/Anchor cotton
  perlé 386
Tapestry wool as follows:

Colour	Appletons	Anchor
Rose pink	754	8366
Heraldic gold	841	8036
Off white	992	8006
Pastel shade		
(× 2)	884	8584
Leaf green		
(1 hank)	421	9112

Finished size
Needlepoint: 39.5 × 12.5 cm
(15½ × 5 in)
Cushion: 39.5 cm (15½ in)
square

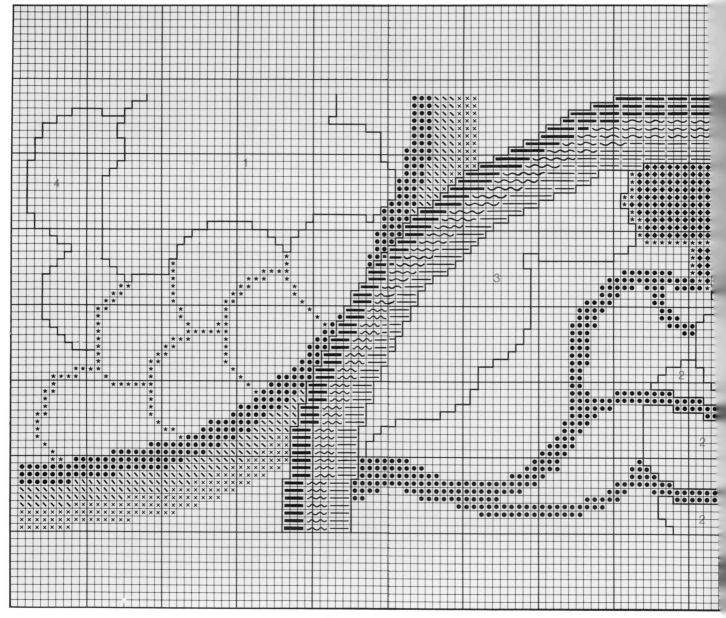

KEY

- ● rose pink 754
- ★ heraldic gold 841
- ☐ off white 992
- ✎ pastel shades 884
- × leaf green 421
- ◆ perlé 746

straight stitches
- — rose pink 754
- ∿ pastel shades 884
- ▬ leaf green 421

1 Byzantine in 421
2 cushion in 841
3 diagonal in 884
4 cushion in 884

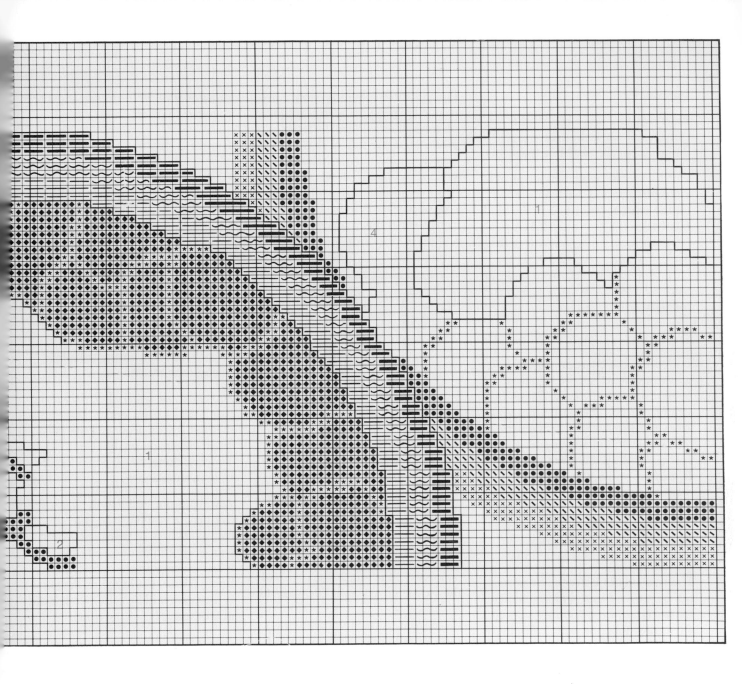

PREPARATION

Bind over the raw edges of the canvas and mark the centre as described in the Skill File (page 16).

Cut 5 cm (2 in) wide bias strips of yellow fabric and use to cover the piping cord as described in the Skill File (page 48). Cut one 42.5 cm (16¾ in) square of green chintz for back. Cut one piece 42.5 × 11 cm (16¾ × 4¼ in) for left front and one piece 42.5 × 22 cm (16¾ × 8⅝ in) for right front.

STITCHING

Following the chart on pages 36–7, work the centre semi-circle first, beginning with the curved lines in straight stitch. Then stitch the pink areas and the outlines of the perlé in tent stitch. Fill in with perlé in cross stitch, working the green area in Byzantine stitch, the mauve in diagonal stitch and the yellow wool in small cushion stitch. Lastly stitch the background in off white in half cross stitch. Follow the Skill File (page 40) for stitch instructions.

The two small quarter circle areas can be worked in a similar manner. However, in these areas the curved lines are stitched in half cross stitch and the mauve area in small cushion stitch.

MAKING UP AND FINISHING

Remove the canvas from the frame and stretch if necessary, as described in the Skill File (page 73).

Pin and stitch covered piping cord to one long edge of each front piece of green chintz. Place the front pieces on either side of the needlepoint with right sides together and stitch down, following previous stitches and against the last row of worked canvas. Trim the canvas edges down to 1.5 cm (⅝ in) and press away from needlepoint (diagram 1).

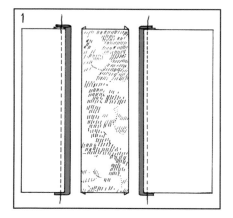

Trim the excess piping cord inside the casing back to the seam allowance lines at top and bottom. Pin and stitch the remainder of the piping to the front panel, positioning the join at the centre of the base edge, see Skill File, page 48.

Place front to cushion back with right sides together; machine stitch around three sides and four corners 1.5 cm (⅝ in) from outer edges leaving a large opening centrally in the base edge. Trim the corners and turn the cover right side out. Insert the cushion pad; turn in the edges of the opening in line with

remainder of the seam and slipstitch together to close.

EXPERIMENTING

This design is ideal for colouring the background canvas and leaving it unstitched, as it would emphasize the raised texturally stitched areas. The colouring can be easily achieved in a variety of methods.

Firstly, use a can of polyurethane spray paint and lightly spray over the canvas. Carefully mask out the areas of canvas which you want to leave plain. Place pieces of paper over the areas, securing the edges firmly with masking tape.

Secondly, use watered down acrylic paints and a paint brush. This method is very accurate especially when colouring small areas. Watered-down fabric paints can be used in the same way.

Always make sure that the paint is dry before you begin to stitch the canvas. Mauve or pale pink would be a good choice of colour and, when making up the cushion, the lining fabric should match the paint colour as it will be seen through the unworked areas of the panel.

As a further experiment, try stitching a border on either side of the needlepoint panel instead of using piping. Tramming as described opposite will give a raised appearance. Attach the tramé threads along the length of the panel, securing at 5 cm (2 in)

intervals, then stitch over them with straight stitches, as in the sample in the photograph. The cushion fabric can then be attached to the edges as before and stitched to the cushion back in the usual way.

Trammed stitch

This is not so much a stitch as a method of leaving threads along the canvas underneath stitches when working over double or Penelope canvas. It ensures that the canvas will be completely covered by the main stitches and makes the needlepoint harder-wearing.

Work horizontally using the same thread as the main stitches, from left to right. On double thread (Penelope) canvas work between the double threads. Make a stitch about 5 cm (2 in) long, going into the canvas at the centre of one intersection. Bring the needle out to the left of the intersection. On single thread canvas, bring the needle out one hole to the left of the previous stitch (diagram 2).

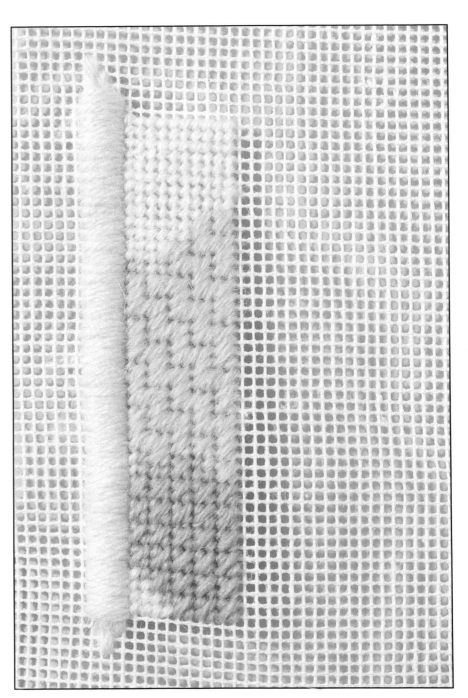

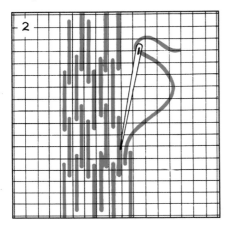

These stitches are best displayed in abstract patterns, where they will not be competing with pictorial designs.

Brick stitch

This stitch is worked over two horizontal threads of canvas, but the stitches are stepped up or down by one canvas thread. Work the rows alternately from right to left and then from left to right. Position the base of the second row of stitches, one stitch length below the preceding row.

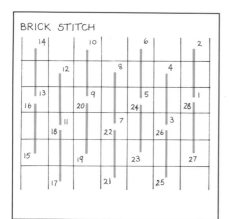

Byzantine stitch

Stitches of similar length are worked in a diagonal pattern across the canvas. Start on the left stitching three diagonal stitches horizontally over two thread intersections. Then work two stitches of the same length vertically under the last stitch. Work two similar stitches horizontally. Repeat in this way across the canvas. In the second row the stitches work alongside the preceding row.

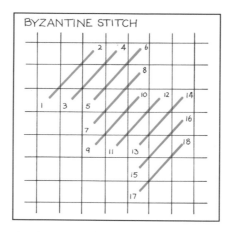

Cushion stitch

This stitch is also known as diagonal satin stitch. The stitches of varying lengths form a square over three or four canvas threads. Work up and down the canvas. Work over 1 intersection, over 2, over 3, over 2 and over 1 again. Slot the second row into the first, placing the longest stitch diagonally beside the shortest stitch in the preceding row. For a different effect reverse the direction of adjoining squares.

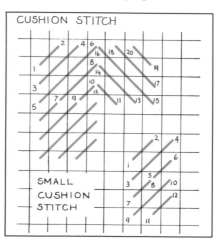

Small cushion stitch

A shorter version with only one long and two short stitches.

Diagonal stitch

A variation of cushion stitch, worked in diagonal bands.

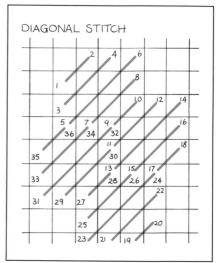

Diagonal mosaic stitch

Made up of a short and a long stitch repeated diagonally over the canvas

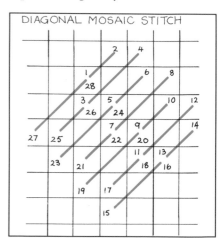

working first down the canvas and then up the canvas. Work over 1 intersection, then 2. In the second row, the long stitches slot beside the short ones of the preceding row.

Diamond eyelet

This is an attractive but large stitch that can be used by itself as a point of decoration in a design. All the stitches radiate from the same hole. Work in a clockwise direction, from the outside, always placing the needle down into the central hole after each stitch.

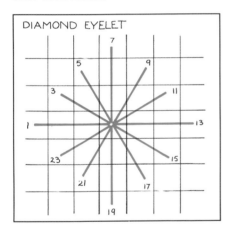

Florentine or bargello

These vertical stitches form a zigzag pattern across the canvas. Worked over two or more threads, descending or ascending in steps, a large number of different patterns can be formed with high peaks and low valleys. By varying the length of the stitches, pinnacled curves are made. Each row follows the preceding one. Extra effect is achieved by using closely-related shades of one or two colours.

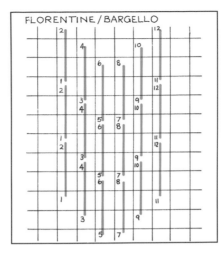

French knots

Bring the needle out of the canvas. Hold the thread taut and wrap round the needle twice, then reinsert in the next hole of the canvas, still holding the thread taut.

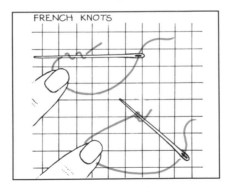

Gobelin or straight stitch

Work the rows alternately from right to left, then left to right. Work vertically over two threads of canvas. The length of stitch can vary. On the second row begin each stitch from one stitch length below the base of the previous stitches.

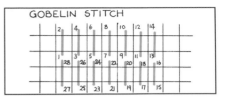

Hungarian stitch

Work the rows alternately from left to right and then from right to left. This stitch consists of groups of three stitches repeated over the canvas. Work the set over 2 horizontal threads, 4 and 2 again. Miss one hole and begin the next set of stitches. In the next row, work backwards so the long stitches are in the gap of the preceding row.

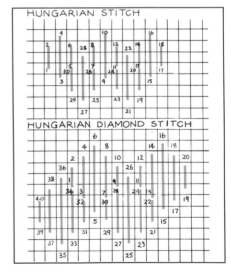

Hungarian diamond

A larger version of Hungarian stitch made up of five stitches, Work over 2 threads, 4 threads, 6 threads, 4 threads and 2 threads. Miss a hole and then work the next set. Fit the next row in between as before.

ROSE-COVERED FOOTSTOOL

Traditional Victorian cabbage roses are stitched over a trellis background for this footstool. The life-like appearance of the flowers is achieved by careful grading of the shades.

To bring this old-fashioned design up to date four to five light subtle yarn colours have been used for each flower. The leaves and background are stitched in dark blues and greens to provide a subdued background that lifts the flowers. Roses are traditionally red and pink, but blends of yellow or pale mauves would look equally relaxed against this muted background. Glean your inspiration from gardening books or plant catalogues or by matching your wool colours to real flowers. To gain the hard-wearing properties needed for upholstered furniture, work in tent stitch using wool over a 12 hole canvas.

REQUIREMENTS

1 piece of white interlock canvas with 12 holes per 2.5 cm (1 in), 42 cm (16 ½ in) square
Tapestry needle size 20
Masking tape
Frame
25 cm (10 in) diameter footstool, composed of frame and pad
10 mm (⅜ in) staples and staple gun or 10 mm (⅜ in) tacks and hammer
Tapestry wool as follows:

Colour	Appletons	Anchor
Coral	862	8232
Coral	863	8310
Autumn yellow	471	8038
Biscuit brown	762	9424
Off white	992	8006
Peacock blue	643	8876
Peacock blue	645	8880
Bright peacock blue	835	9028
Peacock blue (× 2)	641	8872
Marine blue (× 2)	326	8742

	Anchor	
Flesh tints (× 2)	706	9594
Flesh tints (× 2)	703	8296
Coral (× 2)	861	9532
Marine blue (1 hank + 2 skeins)	324	8738

Finished size
32 cm (12 ½ in) diameter circle

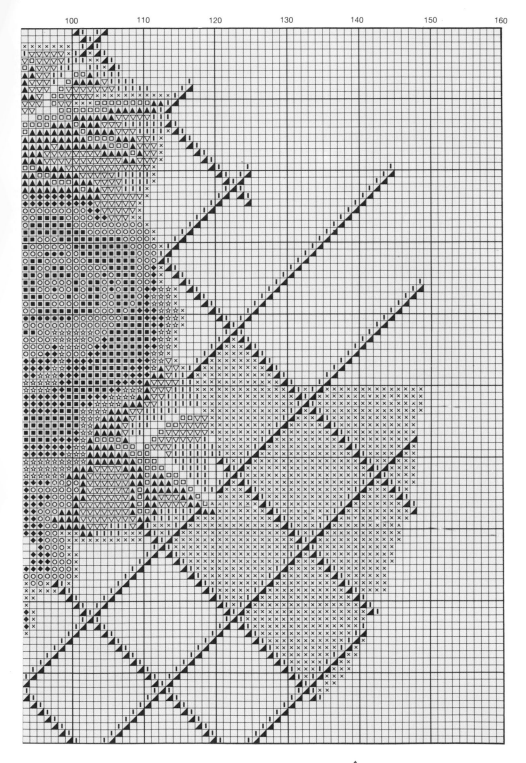

PREPARATION

Bind over the raw canvas edges and mark the centre as described in the Skill File (page 16).

Using a permanent pen attached to a piece of string held at the canvas centre, mark a 16 cm (6¼ in) radius circle (diagram 1). Draw vertical and horizontal lines through the centre of the circle dividing the canvas into four equal quarters.

1

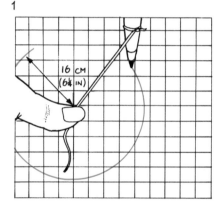

Draw similar lines to the underneath of the footstool pad in the same way, as this will help to position the canvas when the needlepoint is complete.

If you are using an old footstool, make sure that the upholstery is firm and smooth.

Attach the canvas to a frame.

STITCHING

Following the chart on pages 44 and 45, work throughout in tent stitch using 1 strand of tapestry wool. For a footstool of a different size from the one specified, either extend or reduce the background area.

Stitch each rose in turn. Where one area of colour is interrupted by smaller ones, work through the back of the stitches on the wrong side of the canvas and continue stitching on the other side.

Once the roses are complete, finish the trellis and background. The dark blue and pale green lines from bottom left to top right will have to be stitched in back stitch.

MAKING UP AND FINISHING

Remove the needlepoint from the frame and stretch if necessary as described in the Skill File (page 73). Trim the canvas to within 5 cm (2 in) of the worked area.

Remove the pad from the footstool frame. Matching the centre, vertical and horizontal lines, position the needlepoint over the footstool pad. Staple or tack to the underside at these points, pulling the needlepoint taut over the pad (diagram 2).

2

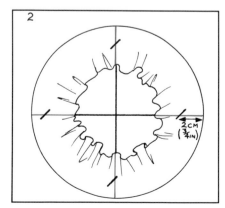

Continue stapling or tacking in between these four points, smoothing the needlepoint over the pad. Form small pleats on the underside to help the canvas lie flat against the base. Snip away any excess canvas. Replace the pad inside the footstool frame.

EXPERIMENTING

Work the background in a different stitch to give an interesting texture, choose from cross stitch, brick stitch, Hungarian stitch, diagonal stitch or kelim, as described in the Skill Files (pages 40–41 and 48).

Beadwork was very popular in Victorian England and was often incorporated in pieces of Berlin woolwork. Try a small amount in the centre of the flowers or at the intersections of the trellis.

Pick small glass beads that are readily available in a variety of colours and shapes. You will need a beading needle, which is a very fine long needle with a narrow eye that can easily fit through the small glass beads. Stitch the beads in place with a strong thread, such as linen or button thread, rubbed through beeswax to give it additional strength. Stitch the beads in place using the same stitch as the needlepoint (diagram 3).

If you use a Penelope or double canvas for the footstool, you can work certain sections in petit point, which means four stitches are worked for one tent stitch, and will

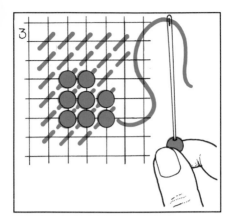

provide minute detail in the shaded areas. For this size canvas use a size 24 needle and one strand of crewel wool (diagram 4).

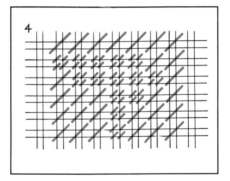

KEY to chart on pages 44-5

- ◆ coral 861
- ● coral 862
- ■ coral 863
- ✶ autumn yellow 471
- + biscuit brown 762
- ☐ off white 992
- ▎ peacock blue 641

- ▽ peacock blue 643
- ▲ peacock blue 645
- ☐ bright peacock blue 835
- ◢ marine blue 326
- × marine blue 324
- ○ flesh tints 706
- ☆ flesh tints 703

A sample piece showing one of the roses with petals worked in beads.

DECORATIVE NEEDLEPOINT STITCHES 2

TRIMMING

Kelim stitch

Work the rows alternately down and up the canvas. Work each stitch diagonally over two intersections of canvas. In the second row, change the direction the stitches.

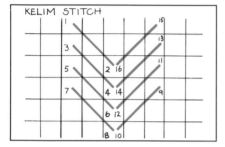

Milanese stitch

Work groups of four diagonal stitches up and down the canvas in the same way as basketweave stitch. In the first row work upwards with each set consisting of a stitch over 1 thread intersection, over 2, over 3 and then over 4. Start the next set over the intersection at the centre of the last stitch. Work the second row downwards with the shortest stitch beside the longest.

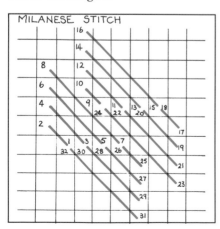

Rhodes stitch

This is another composed stitch worked over a square of eight, six or four threads of canvas. Start by working a diagonal stitch over the canvas and continue making straight stitches across the square of canvas. When the square is complete, a small vertical stitch can be added in the centre.

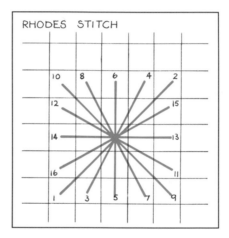

Mistakes

When several stitches have been wrongly worked then these can be carefully unpicked and re-stitched. Use the needle or snip through the stitches with a pair of sharp embroidery scissors. If you accidentally cut one of the canvas threads, this can be repaired by patching. Tack a small square of the same gauge canvas onto the wrong side covering the hole, exactly matching the vertical and horizontal threads of the canvas. Restitch through both layers of canvas, then trim away any excess. The repair should not show on either side.

Piping

Piping is used extensively in soft furnishings and is very easy to make up and insert. Piping cord is available in different thickness, use 3, 4 or 5 for most furnishing projects. To cover piping cord successfully, the covering fabric must be cut on the cross of the fabric. To find the true cross (diagram 1) fold the fabric diagonally so the two edges align and press along the fold.

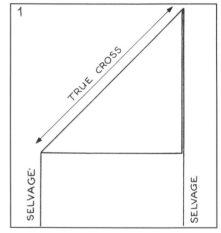

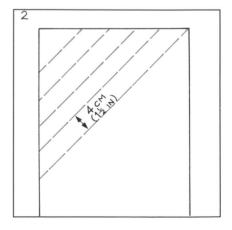

Measure and mark the 4 cm (1½ in) wide strips (diagram 2) parallel to this folded edge. Once the strips have been cut out, join them on the straight of grain (diagram 3) to form the length you need.

Place the piping along the seamline of the fabric with the cord facing inwards and raw edges matching fabric edges (diagram 5). Stitch in place a short distance away from

the cord. Start and finish approximately 5 cm (2 in) either side of the ends of the covered cord which should overlap by about 2.5 cm (1 in).

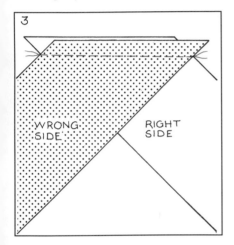

Place the piping cord onto the wrong side of the strip and fold the fabric evenly in half round it; pin and stitch down the strip a short distance away from the cord (diagram 4) using a piping foot on the sewing machine.

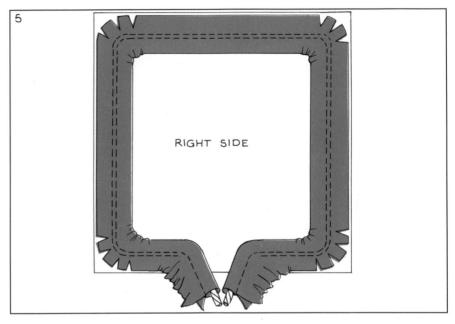

To join the ends together to fit round a cushion cover, trim the fabric and cord ends; unstitch the piping seam and stitch the fabric strips together; trim the seam. Unravel the cord ends and snip alternate strands from each end. Intertwine them (diagram 6) again

and bind with sewing thread to form a good join (diagram 7). Refold the strip of piping fabric over the join and stitch. Place the cushion back over the front with right sides together. Stitch all round as close as possible to the cord, to cover the previous stitching lines.

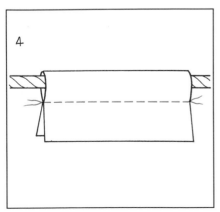

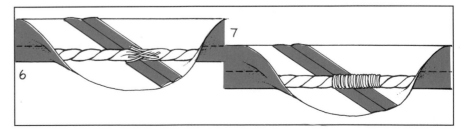

SILK FLORENTINE CUSHION

One of the most popular styles of needlepoint is
Florentine work. Combine pure silk threads
with raw silk fabric in this picturesque style
to create a luxurious cushion.

This cushion has a central panel stitched in a
four-way Florentine or Bargello design
worked on a fine 18 hole canvas using 5
strands of Madeira silk embroidery threads.
The steps of the stitches vary to create both
gradual curves and steeper lines. Four shades
of apricot have been selected to give the classic
graduated shading.

The overall design is achieved by four
triangular quarters, stitched at right angles to
each other. A non-symmetrical pattern has
been chosen to produce an exciting and
interesting result, but still in keeping with the
restful curves of the Florentine work. The
success depends on the accuracy with which
you place each stitch.

REQUIREMENTS

1 piece of interlock white
canvas with 18 holes per
2.5 cm (1 in), 30 cm (12 in)
square
Tapestry needle size 22
Masking tape
1 m (1 yd) apricot silk
2 m (2¼ yds) piping cord
Matching sewing thread
Cushion pad 38 cm (15 in)
square

Madeira pure silk thread as
follows: 5 skeins each of
0306, 0305, 0403, 0303
1 m (1 yd) decorative cord

Finished size
Needlepoint square: 20 cm
(8 in) square
Cushion: 38 cm (15 in)
square

PREPARATION

Bind over the raw edges of canvas and mark the centre as described in the Skill File (page 16). Draw a 20 cm (8 in) square centrally on the canvas, following horizontal and vertical threads of canvas. Draw diagonal lines crossing the centre dividing the canvas into four triangles.

It is important that the first row of stitching is correct, as all the other rows follow on from this row, so draw in a grid of vertical and horizontal lines every 10 threads across the canvas. These will match with the grid lines on the chart. A frame is not required for this project.

Cut two pieces of silk 43 cm (17 in) square. Make up a 2 m (2¼ yd) length of apricot silk covered piping, see Skill File (page 48) using silk thread.

STITCHING

Start with the top complete row (see chart opposite) and work from left to right, using straight stitches over three threads (page 41). From this row fill in the area above, then work towards the centre. When you have completed the first triangle, turn the canvas and work the next. Repeat, until all are stitched.

MAKING UP AND FINISHING

Trim the excess canvas to 1.5 cm (⅝ in). Turn to the wrong side and press. Trim corners. With the right side up, centre the worked canvas

on one of the silk squares and tack carefully in position. Machine stitch as close as possible to the edge, leaving a 1 cm (⅜ in) gap in the centre of the base edge.

Attach the piping to the outside edges of this front panel, pin and tack. Place this panel to second piece of silk with right sides together; machine stitch around the cover 1.5cm (⅝ in) from outer edges and leaving a large opening in the centre of base edge. Trim the corners and turn the cover right side out.

Stitch the decorative cord carefully around the outer edges of the worked canvas square, beginning and ending in the 1 cm (⅜ in) gap (diagram 1). Insert the cushion pad. Turn in the edges of the opening in line with remainder of the seam and slipstitch together to close.

EXPERIMENTING

This stitched triangle is extremely versatile for making other cushion

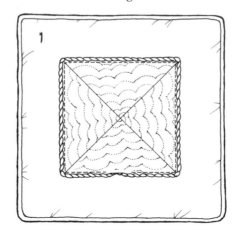

patterns. Try repeating the side triangles only to make an interlocking design (diagram 2) for a decorative panel. To gain an overall pattern repeat the existing design four times. Change the

2

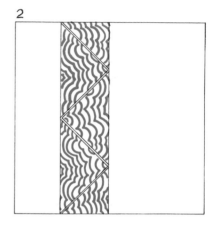

position of the triangles to form a central diamond. The stitching lines from these variations will produce very interesting results.

Alternatively, these separately stitched triangles could be appliquéd to a base fabric using an iron-on bonding web. Turn under the raw edges of the canvas for 1.5 cm (⅝ in) and iron onto the bonding web. Peel off the protective backing and iron onto the main fabric. When all the triangles are in place, the folded canvas edges can be machined all round with a closely-worked satin stitch. Triangles the same size as the pattern can be used, alternatively the pattern can be stitched onto a finer size of canvas to produce smaller triangles.

KEY
0306
0305
0403
0303

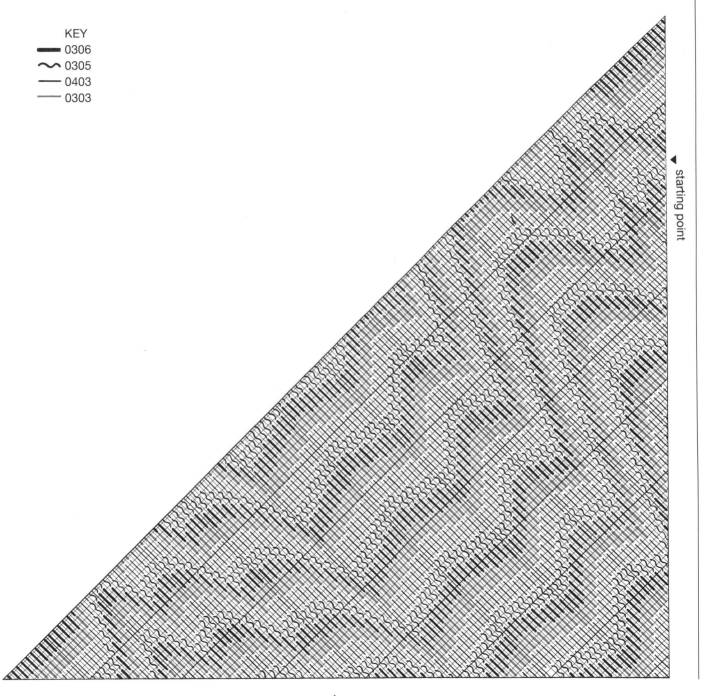

▶ starting point

SAMPLER PINCUSHION

This pincushion records a wide variety of different stitches.
Worked in muted Autumnal shades the finished result is
trimmed with decorative cord and corner tassels.

Crewel wool is used throughout this project. The stitching is begun with 3 strands of the same colour, then 3 strands of darker and lighter shades are mixed together in the needle (two of one shade plus one of another), creating fascinating colour mixes. A large scallop shell was used as inspiration for the natural mix of colours. Surprisingly, when this was closely inspected it was found to contain a number of unrelated shades, which were translated into this attractive colour combination. Worked on 14 hole canvas it was possible to include twelve different stitches in the randomly-shaped areas and surround them with half cross stitch to fill any gaps between the different textures.

REQUIREMENTS

1 piece of antique interlock
    canvas with 14 holes per
    2.5 cm (1 in), 19 cm
    (7½ in) square
Tapestry needle size 22
Masking tape
1 piece of matching fabric
    12 cm (5 in) square
Matching sewing thread
15 cm (6 in) hoop frame
Small amount of suitable
    filling

Crewel wool as follows:

Colour	Appletons	Paterna
Flame red	206	871
Flame red	203	486
Bright terracotta	221	490
Flesh tints	701	494
Flesh tints	702	494
Coral	861	855

Finished size
9 cm (3½ in) square

PREPARATION

Bind over the raw edges of canvas and mark the centre as described in the Skill File (page 16). Attach the canvas to a hoop frame. Make up a 42 cm (16½ in) length of cord using crewel wool or in matching stranded cottons and make four tassels as described below.

STITCHING

Use 3 strands of crewel wool for all the stitches, except cross stitch, Rhodes stitch and diamond eyelet; for these stitches use 2 strands of crewel wool. Follow the chart key opposite for details of colour mixes and stitches.

Start with the Hungarian diamond stitch in the centre and work outwards. The stitches used are Hungarian stitch, Hungarian diamond, diagonal mosaic, cross, diamond eyelet, Milanese, kelim, Rhodes, Byzantine, Gobelin, cushion and half cross as described in the Skill Files (pages 40, 41 and 48) .

MAKING UP AND FINISHING

Remove the needlepoint from the hoop and trim the canvas to within 1.5 cm (⅝ in) of the stitching. Press on the wrong side over a damp cloth. Place the needlepoint and fabric with right sides together; machine stitch around three sides and four corners leaving a central opening. Trim down the seam allowance and turn right side out.

Fill firmly, turn in the edges of the opening in line with the remainder of the seam and slipstitch across the opening to close. Attach cord and tassels as described opposite.

EXPERIMENTING

Look at other natural objects for ready-made colour schemes, for example, fruit and vegetables, flowers and leaves, birds and animals, fungi, insects or minerals. Begin by looking closely at the object and selecting threads in the exact colours. Wind these around a piece of cardboard, if possible in the same proportions as in the object. This will be the base for your needlepoint colour scheme. You can see the effective result in the example here of a cauliflower and subsequent needlepoint pincushion. The equivalent colour numbers to the shell are:

Colour	Appletons	Anchor
Leaf green	425	206
Early English green	543	203
Sea green	401	221
Off-white	992	701
Pastel shade	872	702
Leaf green	421	861
Heraldic gold	841	472

Also perlé in cream/yellow and DMC stranded cotton 912.

The perlé cotton and stranded cottons have been used to highlight certain areas. Try experimenting further with silk, metallic threads or machine embroidery cottons.

Twisted cord

Measure and cut the strands, ten times the finished length; tie the ends together into a circle. Form into two circles and place over two pencils with the knot at one end (diagram 1). Twist the pencils in

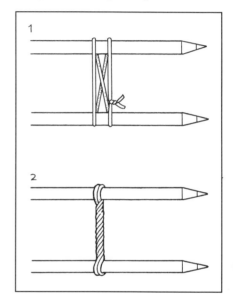

opposite directions until the threads are very tightly twisted (diagram 2). Fold up one pencil to the other, still pulling the threads taut, then let go and the cords will twist together. Remove the pencils.

The cords can be made thicker or thinner by using more or fewer threads.

Stitching cord

Use a small curved needle and strong thread, such as linen or button thread. Start with a slip knot and work from right to left. Stitch through the centre of the cord, then

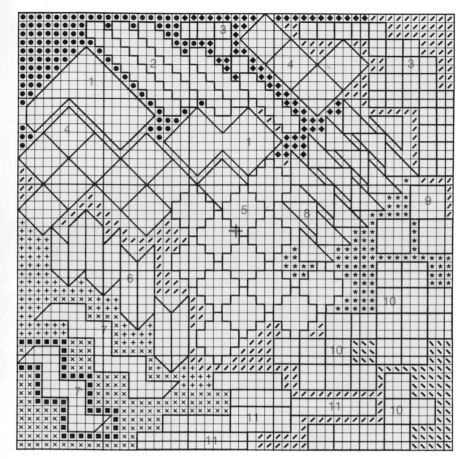

KEY

- flesh tints 701
- ◆ flesh tints 702
- ✔ flame red 203
- ■ flame red 206
- ✳ bright terracotta 221 (2 strands) + 702 (1)
- + 203 (2 strands) + 206 (1)
- × 203 (1 strand) + 206 (2)
- ↘ 221 (2 strands) + coral 861 (1)

1 Hungarian
2 diagonal mosaic
3 cross
4 diamond eyelet
5 Hungarian diamond
6 kelim
7 Byzantine
8 Milanese
9 Rhodes
10 cushion
11 gobelin (straight)

diagonally through the fabric behind to the bottom edge of the cord; repeat. Stitches should be approximately 1 cm (⅜ in) apart.

Take care not to untwist or over twist the cord while stitching.

Tassels

Cut a number of yarn lengths depending on the thickness of the yarn being used and the size of tassel required. Either keep to one colour or mix different shades together. Fold in half and use one

crewel thread to wrap around 1 cm (⅜ in) from the fold. Wrap round anti-clockwise leaving an end protruding at the bottom and the loop protruding at the top (diagrams 3a and b). Thread the end of the yarn through the loop and pull the end at the bottom downwards, so that the loop disappears behind the wrapped thread (diagram 3c). Trim the ends.

Use approximately thirty 12 cm (5 in) lengths of crewel wool for each tassel.

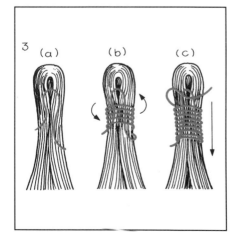

CHINESE CUSHION

Translate the design from a piece of china onto canvas and
create an oriental cushion. With a repeating central pattern,
there is an inner border complete with
Chinese letters.

The pattern created for this cushion has been taken from a piece of Chinese china. The design is composed of three different segments, a central panel repeated four times, an inner border displaying Chinese lettering and an outer border of the background pattern. Each section is separated with a band of straight stitching or Gobelin stitch. Tent stitch has been used to gain an even tension because of the many small irregular lines of pattern. This is an ideal design for reproducing on a larger gauge canvas for a more extensive project such as a rug. Alternatively the border could be used by itself, worked round a central square of textured stitching.

REQUIREMENTS

1 piece of white interlock canvas with 12 holes per 2.5 cm (1 in), 51 cm (20 in) square

Tapestry needle size 20

Masking tape

Frame

Set square or protractor

1 piece of turquoise fabric 44 cm (17½ in) square plus extra for the piping

2.5 m (2¾ yd) of piping cord

Matching sewing thread

40 cm (16 in) square cushion pad

Tapestry wool as follows:

Colour	Appletons	Anchor
Dull marine blue	323	0705
Rose pink	751	8392
Peacock blue	643	8876
Peacock blue	644	8878

Flame red (× 2)	204	8324
Pastel shade (× 2)	877	8294
Rose pink (× 2)	144	8416
Grey/green (1 hank)	352	9058
Turquoise (2 hanks)	524	8916

Finished size
40 cm (16 in) square

PREPARATION

Bind over the raw edges of canvas and mark the centre as described in the Skill File (page 16). Draw vertical and horizontal lines dividing the canvas into four equal quarters. Draw diagonal lines from the corners to the centre, further dividing the canvas into eight, using a set square or protractor to ensure 45° angles. Finally mark the two bands of Gobelin stitch to act as a guideline.

Attach the canvas to a frame as described in the Skill File (page 17).

STITCHING

Work the design throughout in tent stitch using 1 strand of tapestry wool (see key and chart right and on page 61).

Start in the centre, stitching the motif first. Work along the diagonal line, stitching the flower. When the four quarter motifs have been completed, stitch the two border bands. The small yellow motifs on the background should be completed before the turquoise areas.

MAKING UP AND FINISHING

Remove the needlepoint from the frame and stretch if necessary as described in the Skill File (page 73). Trim the canvas to within 1.5 cm (⅝ in) of the worked areas.

Make up covered piping cord in turquoise, as described in the Skill File (page 48). Pin and stitch the piping to the fabric, positioning the join at the centre of the base edge. Place needlepoint and fabric with right sides together; machine stitch three sides and four corners, leaving a large opening in base edge. Trim corners and turn right side out. Insert cushion pad, turn in the edges of the opening in line with remainder of the seam and slipstitch together to close.

EXPERIMENTING

In keeping with many oriental items, this cushion would look beautiful stitched with silk threads. For this unique lustre use a four-stranded silk floss which is available in a wide variety of colours, or a twisted non-divisible silk thread, available both in fine and medium thickness.

An interesting product highly suitable for use here is waste canvas. In this technique, you stitch through a piece of waste canvas fixed to a piece of fabric and once completed pull away the canvas threads leaving the evenly-stitched motif on the fabric. The flower motif or any part of this design can be stitched onto a fabric, such as velvet or cotton chintz instead of canvas.

Cut a small piece of canvas, position on the chosen fabric and tack in place, working from the centre outwards. Carefully stitch the design in cross stitch through both canvas and fabric, working from the centre outwards. Pull the stitches slightly tighter than usual as these will become loose when the canvas is removed. You may find it necessary to change to a chenille needle as it has a sharp point. It is very important, however, not to pierce the canvas threads with this needle. When the motif is complete, remove the tacking stitches and trim away excess canvas. Remove the canvas threads one at a time with a pair of tweezers. If you find this difficult, carefully dampen to soften the canvas threads.

KEY
★ dull marine blue 323
▼ rose pink 751
○ peacock blue 643
✎ peacock blue 644
+ flame red 204
● pastel shade 877
■ rose pink 144
× grey/green 352
□ turquoise 524
straight stitches in grey/green 352

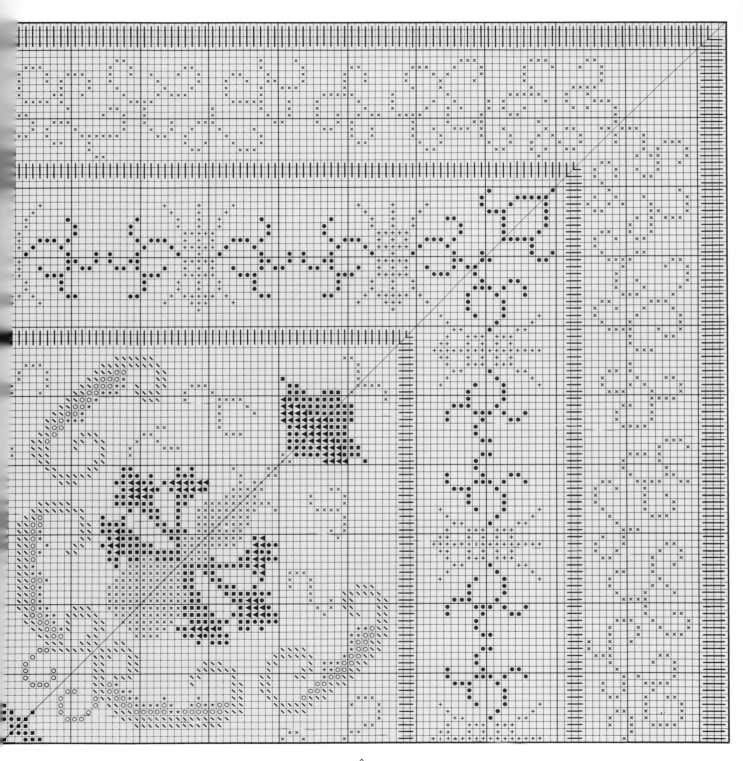

NURSERY TIME PICTURE

A charming picture to hang on a child's bedroom wall worked
in simple bright colours. Stitch clown and his best friend teddy
in a variety of simple textured stitches.

This design is stitched entirely in stranded cotton to give a slightly shiny appearance. To give the picture soft shading, some of the colours have been intermixed.

Texture has also been introduced by using French knots for the clown's hair, by using cross stitch for the balloons and by adding a tassel on the clown's hat. The solid background areas have also been given added interest as they are stitched in small cushion stitch in a mixture of pinks. The border is worked in three closely related colours.

REQUIREMENTS

1 piece of white interlock canvas with 14 holes per 2.5 cm (1 in), 29 × 32 cm (11½ × 12½ in)
Tapestry needle size 22
Masking tape
1 piece of mounting board 19 × 21.5 cm (7½ × 8½ in)
1 piece of 2 oz polyester wadding 19 × 21.5 cm (7½ × 8½ in)
Set square

Strong thread, such as crochet cotton
Craft knife, steel rule and cutting board
1 picture frame 19 × 17 cm (7½ × 6¾ in)
Stranded cotton as follows:

Colour	DMC	Anchor
Light pink	948	778
Pale mauve	211	342
Sand	950	4146
Pink/beige	3772	914

Mauve	553	98
Dark pink	601	63
Purple	550	101
Bright pink (× 2)	603	62
Beige	739	366
Pale apricot	945	881
Black		
White		
Pale pink (× 2)	819	271
Medium pink (× 3)	605	60

Finished size
19 × 17 cm (7½ × 6¾ in)

PREPARATION

Bind over the raw edges of canvas and mark centre as described in the Skill File (page 16).

STITCHING

Use 6 strands of stranded cotton throughout, except for the areas of cross stitch. Use 4 strands for cross stitch. Work in half cross stitch except for the areas keyed in on the chart opposite. Start stitching the balloon strings, then stitch clown's spots, buttons and centre suit line, ruff, hair, hat, mouth, nose, eyes and face. Outline the bricks and letters, then work the background.

Stitch the frieze border, numbers and background. Stitch the balloons, clown's feet and the final background.

Make a tassel out of a mixture of pink stranded cottons (page 57) and attach to the top of the clown's hat.

Complete by stitching the border, working three rows of straight stitches over two canvas threads.

Use 8 strands of thread and work the three rows in 603 (62), 605 (60) and 819 (271).

MAKING UP AND FINISHING

Attach the piece of wadding to the mounting board with a few spots of glue, then trim the edges level with the board. Place the wadded side of the mounting board centrally on the wrong side of the needlepoint and mount as described in the Skill File (page 72). Frame as desired.

EXPERIMENTING

Try the alternative border pattern charted in diagram 1. Use three strands of embroidery cotton and follow the chart for the order of the stitching. The first nine diagonal stitches are worked in 604 (51) and the next nine stitches in the opposite direction in 605 (60).

Continue, alternating directions and colours until complete.

This design could be stitched for a cushion panel, either on the same size canvas or on a 12 or 10 hole canvas. The 12 hole canvas would produce a piece 23 × 20 cm (9 × 8 in) and the 10 hole canvas a 28 × 24 cm (11 × 9½ in) picture. Soft aquas, blues or pale yellows would make an attractive deviation from pink, or why not use the waste canvas technique and stitch either the clown or the teddy onto a plain fabric and turn it into curtains, clothes bag, lampshade or even a small decorative table cloth to make a matching nursery set.

KEY

◆ white
☆ pale pink 819
✎ medium pink 605
× bright pink 603
□ dark pink 601
● 601 (3 strands) + 603 (3)
○ 605 (3 strands) + 603 (3)
▼ 603 (2 strands) + 950 (4)
▲ 603 (4 strands) + 950 (2)
▮ beige 739
▽ sand 950
Z 950 (3 strands) + 3772 (3)
+ pink/beige 3772
✐ pale mauve 211
□ 211 (3 strands) + white (3)
★ 553 (2 strands) + 211 (4)
▲ 550 (2 strands) + 553 (2)
◢ purple 550
▨ mauve 553
■ black
— light pink 948
• white (5 strands) + 211 (1)
○ pale apricot 945

A clown's hair, French knots in 950
B background, small cushion stitch in 605 (3 strands) + 819 (3)
C frieze border, straight stitch in 211
D balloons, cross stitch (colours as key)

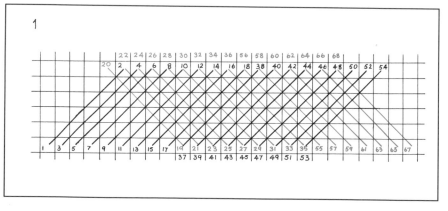

1

ART NOUVEAU SEAT

An elegant corner chair is transformed with a new canvaswork seat. Florentine motifs and zigzags combine to make a fascinating pattern for this typical Art Nouveau chair.

The flowing lines of the side panels, so typical of this design period, have been effectively used for the stitch pattern. Areas of both curved and angular zigzags link up these connecting motifs. A two-way pattern has been incorporated in this design, as corner chairs do not have a well defined front and back. The chart is for the right-hand side of the seat and merely needs reversing for the left side, while an interesting pattern emerges along the adjoining line. The Florentine stitches are worked over three threads in 4 strands of crewel wool producing a hard-wearing cover. By using seven shades a gradual progression of colour is achieved across the seat.

REQUIREMENTS

	Colour	Appletons	Paterna
1 piece of antique interlock canvas with 12 holes per 2.5 cm (1 in), 51 cm (20 in) square	1 hank of each of the following:		
	Flame red	202	406
	Flame red	203	486
Tapestry needle size 20	Flame red	204	485
Masking tape	Flame red	205	872
Frame	Flame red	206	871
10 mm ($\frac{3}{8}$ in) fine tacks and hammer	Flame red	207	870
	Flame red	208	870
1.5m ($1\frac{3}{4}$ yd) of trimming	Flesh tints	701	494
Clear fabric adhesive			
Gimp pins	**Finished size**		
Crewel wool as follows:	37 cm ($14\frac{1}{2}$ in) square		

PREPARATION

Bind over the raw edges of canvas and mark the centre as described in the Skill File (page 16). Label the top and bottom. Draw a line diagonally through the centre point from the bottom left to the top right, dividing the square into two equal triangles. Mark in grid lines horizontally and vertically every 10 lines. These can be matched to the grid lines on the chart to ensure accurate stitching. Attach the canvas to a frame, as described in the Skill File (page 17).

Check that the upholstery on the chair seat is both firm and comfortable. It should be covered with calico.

As this is a repeat pattern, it is very easily adapted to fit any size of chair seat. The distance marked is one pattern repeat crosswise and can be multiplied as many times as is necessary to fit another seat. The depth of the pattern section shown (diagram 1) is 28 cm (11 in) and can be made to fit another seat by

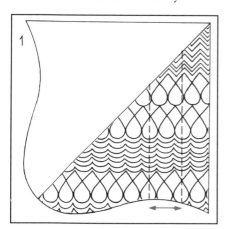

repeating the zigzag rows as necessary (diagram 2).

2

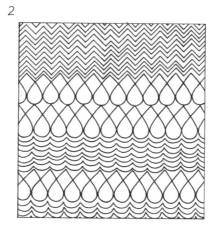

Alternatively, the front of the pattern could be extended so that the rows of connecting motifs are positioned in the centre (diagram 3).

3

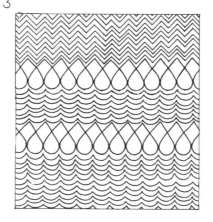

STITCHING

Work in Florentine stitch (page 41) and follow the chart on pages 70–1. Start by stitching the outline of the three complete rows of connecting motifs. Fill these in, then move

onto the areas in between. For areas A and B, work the stitches in direction 1, for area C, work in direction 2 (diagram 4). This ensures that the needle will come up in an empty hole and down in a stitched one. All the stitches, except the fillers, are worked over three threads, with steps of 1 or 2 threads.

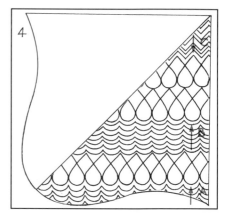

MAKING UP AND FINISHING

Remove the canvas from the frame. It is unlikely to need stretching as all the stitches are straight. Matching centres, place the canvas over the chair seat and temporary tack (hammer the tack only halfway into the frame) at the four corners, taking care to keep the stitching rows parallel to the chair frame. Fill the areas in between with temporary tacks approximately 2 cm (¾ in) apart. Take care not to pull the canvas sideways. The canvas should fit the seat without any puckers at the edges or corners. Make sure that the tension of the

canvas is firm on the seat; check by
running your hand back and forth.

Carefully hammer the tacks in fully:
to avoid damaging the surrounding
wood it is advisable to use a punch.
Trim the excess canvas as close as
possible to the tack heads using
very sharp scissors or a craft knife.

Finish by glueing on the trimming;
a scroll gimp is preferable here, as
this will stretch to fit snugly around
the curved front shape. Turn under
the raw edges diagonally and butt
up at the back corner (diagram 5).
Hold in place with four gimp pins.

EXPERIMENTING

For the more adventurous, use this

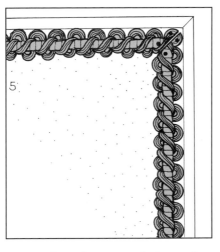

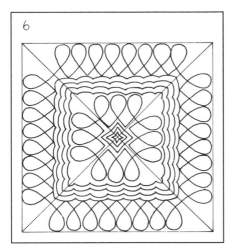

pattern for a four-way design as for
the Florentine cushion square on
page 51. Divide your chair seat
dimensions into 4 equal triangles

and choose a section of the pattern
to fit one of these (diagram 6).
Or try a regular pattern as in the
chart below, which uses 7 shades.

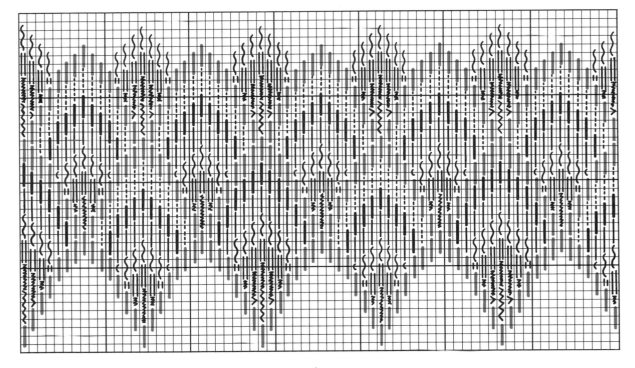

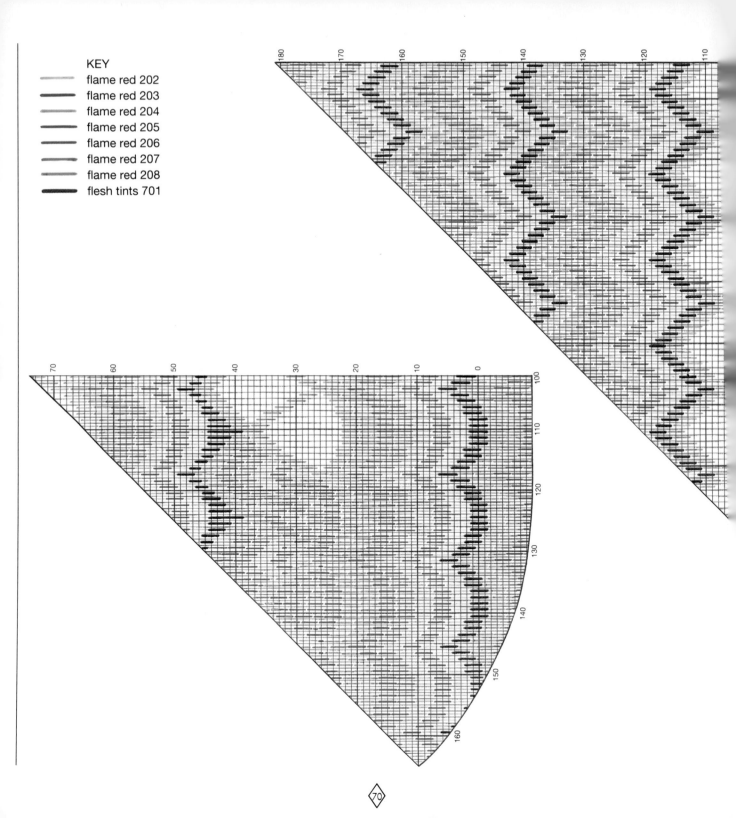

KEY
flame red 202
flame red 203
flame red 204
flame red 205
flame red 206
flame red 207
flame red 208
flesh tints 701

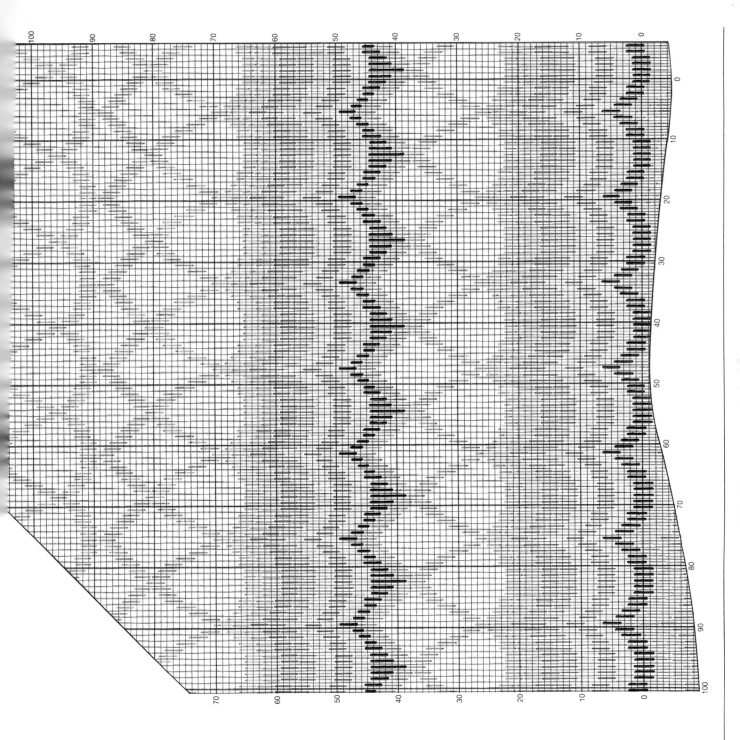

Mitring Corners of Canvas

When a piece of needlepoint is not framed or laced over a board, the canvas edges need to be turned under and neatened. In the majority of cases, it is enough to turn the edges under along the final row of stitching and glue or hand stitch a piece of lining over the back.

Turn under the raw edges of the lining before stitching it to the canvas.

If the canvas is bulky the corners will lie flatter if they are mitred. Cut away the corner of the canvas, 1 cm (⅜ in) from the stitching (diagram 1). Fold this edge

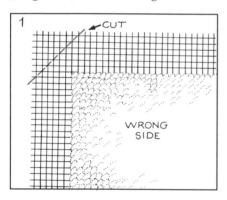

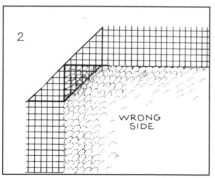

diagonally over the stitched corner (diagram 2). Fold the sides inwards so that they meet, making a diagonal join. Stitch across the join to hold it together (diagram 3).

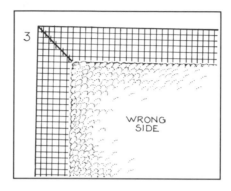

Mounting the Canvas

When the finished piece of needlepoint is to be framed, it must first be mounted on a piece of card or hardboard.

Place the mounting board centrally on the wrong side of the stitched canvas and, using household pins (these will need to be tacks if the mount is hardboard), carefully pin the canvas to the edge of the board along the top edge, following a straight thread. Repeat with the base edge, stretching the canvas taut. Pin the canvas to each side edge in the same way and then check that the canvas is straight and taut.

Trim the excess canvas down to 4 cm (1½ in) and then begin lacing. Use a strong thread, such as crochet cotton, and a sharp needle. Start in the centre of one side and make

long herringbone stitches back and forth across the back of the board (diagram 4). Repeat, to lace the top and base edges together in the same way, tucking under each corner

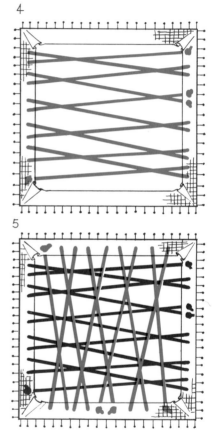

(diagram 5). Once the canvas is securely laced the pins can be removed and the mounted picture can be framed.

Hanging a Needlepoint Picture

For a simple wall hanging, turn under the canvas edges, mitring the corners. Place a piece of lining to the wrong side of the canvas, tucking under the raw edges to neaten. Slipstitch all round the hanging, leaving an opening at the top of each side to insert a length of dowel. Cut a length of dowel 10 cm (4 in) longer that the wall hanging. Slot through the openings. Tie a length of decorative cord round the protruding ends and hang.

For a picture, place a piece of lining to the wrong side of the canvas, turning in the raw edges. Fold back the lining across the centre and lockstitch the lining to the back of the canvas. Repeat on either side of the centre, so the lining is held against the canvas. Slipstitch the outer edges of lining to outer edge of canvas. Handsew a curtain ring centrally to the back of the picture, or if the picture is very wide, sew two rings in place, evenly spaced across the back of the picture.

Blocking and Stretching
This is the method used to straighten the canvas back to its original shape after it has been stitched. It is only necessary when the stitching has distorted the canvas, but it can also be used to freshen up a piece of needlepoint.

Use a clean piece of wood larger than the finished canvas. Cover with a layer of blotting paper, then lay the needlepoint face down over the blotting paper. If you have a paper template of the outline of the finished stitching, place this over

the blotting paper underneath the needlepoint.

Spray water over the canvas to dampen it. Secure the unstitched edges of the canvas around the edge with upholsterers tacks or drawing pins. Begin by pinning the corners, matching these with the template, use a set square to make sure you

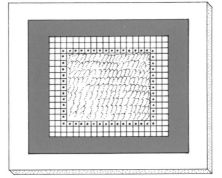
6

gain straight and right-angled edges. Snip into any selvage edges at intervals so that the canvas can stretch evenly. Place the remaining tacks or pins between the corners, 1–2 cm ($\frac{3}{8}$–$\frac{3}{4}$ in) apart, again matching against the template (diagram 6).

Allow the canvas to dry thoroughly. If the canvas is still distorted, repeat the process. Depending on how wet the canvas becomes, drying may take a few days.

Finally, if the canvas was badly distorted, it is a good idea to fix the corrected shape by brushing the wrong side with a thin layer of wallpaper paste. Allow this to dry before removing the canvas.

Care of Canvas
When you are not working on the canvas always roll it up rather than folding it, which would eventually distort the canvas threads. Store the rolled-up canvas in a clean cloth or bag to protect it.

Joining Canvas
It is possible to join two pieces of canvas together to make up a larger width. To join two pieces, first trim off the selvages of the adjoining pieces. Overlap the two edges by 3 or 4 vertical threads, matching the canvas exactly together. Using a strong thread, oversew the canvas together down each overlapping vertical thread (diagram 7).

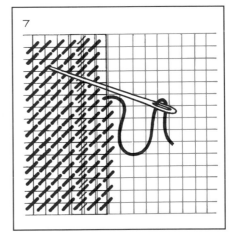
7

The needlepoint can then be worked over the join as if it is one piece of canvas.

TULIP RUG

Brighten up the home with this stylish Spring-time rug embroidered in shades of apricot and leaf green. These pretty tulips are surrounded by a green-crossed border.

Rug wool is used to give both an attractive and hard-wearing surface. Although this is a relatively large project, easy work has been made of it by using a 7 hole canvas, which is still a small enough gauge to allow shading in the tulips. And, if when the rug is completed, you feel that this work of art is too good to walk on, use it as a wall hanging instead.

REQUIREMENTS

1 piece of polished interlock rug canvas with 7 holes to 2.5 cm (1 in), 117 × 84 cm (46 × 33 in)
Tapestry needle size 16 or 18
Masking tape
Large frame
1 piece of carpet felt or curtain interlining 100 × 69 cm (40 × 27 in)
1 piece of hessian 107 × 74 cm (42 × 29 in)

Carpet thread and curved needle and pins
2-ply rug wool as follows:
drab green (100 gm)
cream (100 gm)
7 shades of orange (1 hank)
bright green (1 hank)
dark green (700 gm)

Finished size
100 × 69 cm (40 × 27 in)

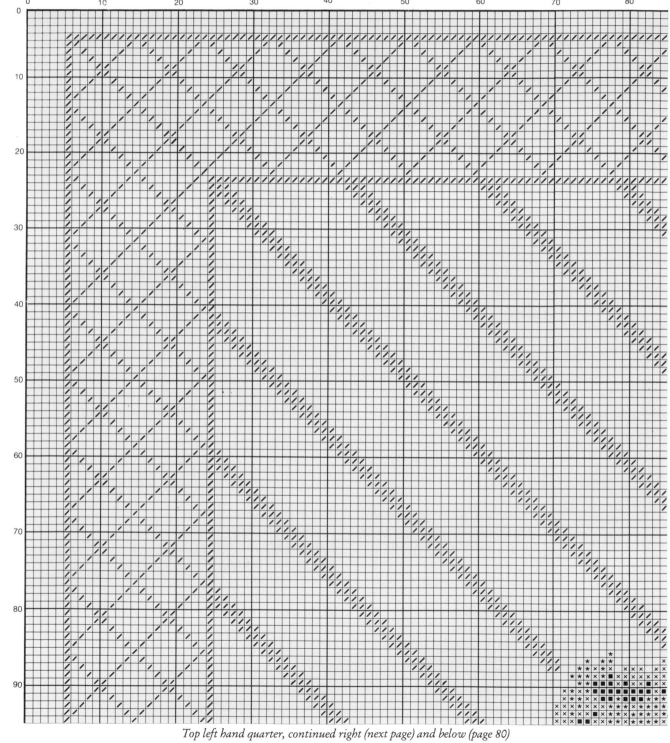

Top left hand quarter, continued right (next page) and below (page 80)

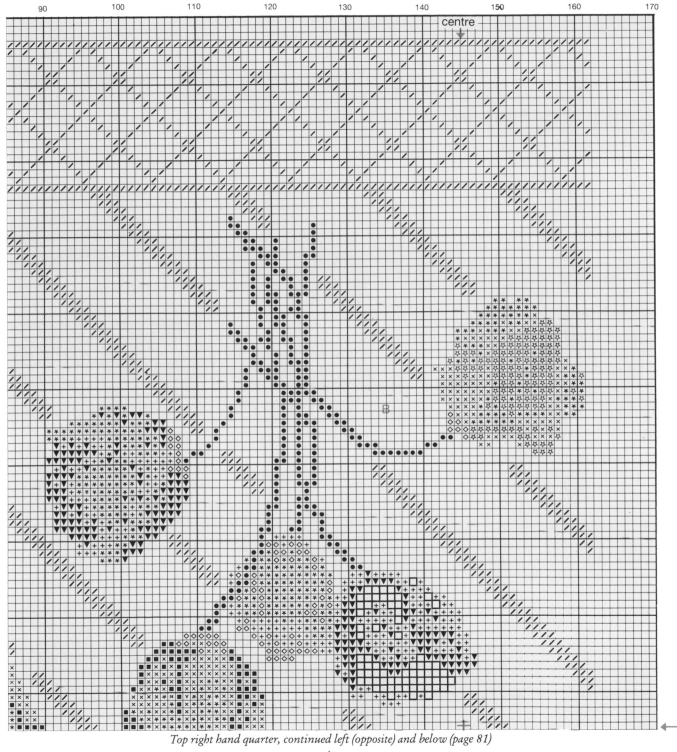

Top right hand quarter, continued left (opposite) and below (page 81)

CONSTRUCTION

PREPARATION

Bind over the raw edges of canvas and find the centre as described in the Skill File (page 16). Draw horizontal and vertical lines through the centre point.

Attach the canvas to the frame as described in the Skill File (page 17). This will not only help to keep the stitching tension even, but also prevent distortion of the canvas, as it is difficult to block and stretch such a large item.

STITCHING

Use 2 strands of rug wool throughout. Start with the border, stitching all the bright green lines, working in basketweave stitch (page 32) and backstitch (page 33) for the diagonals and half cross stitch (page 32) for the edges.

Next stitch the tulips using half cross stitch, the exact position of the tulips is easily counted from the borders.

The chart given on pages 76–7 and 80–1 is for half the rug, so once tulips A and B have been stitched, repeat A, following the starting position shown on the centre line. Tulip B can then be stitched using A as a guide for positioning.

For the background, stitch the diagonal lines first, using basketweave stitch, then fill in with dark green, using half cross stitch or basketweave stitch. The latter will give a very solid underside to the

rug but half cross stitch will be easier on the hands.

MAKING UP AND FINISHING

Remove the canvas from the frame and block if necessary. Fold under the unworked canvas on all sides, so that the last row of stitching is nearly underneath. This will ensure that there is no exposed canvas showing through on the right side. Trim the turnings to 4 cm (1½ in) and using a small curved needle and carpet thread, slipstitch these edges to the back of the canvas, mitring the corners.

Pin the padding to the wrong side of the canvas and trim down to within 6 mm (¼ in) of the edge and stitch. Place the hessian centrally over the padding, turn under the edges in line with the canvas and slipstitch to the canvas all round (diagram 1).

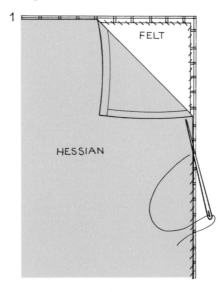

FELT

HESSIAN

EXPERIMENTING

This rug can be made longer, even into a runner by adding two or more bunches of tulips to the length. The width can also be altered in the same way.

To add fringing to the ends of this rug, work as follows. Firstly, on the two short sides, fold under the canvas, so that the first unworked thread is on the fold (diagram 2). The fringing will be attached to this line of holes.

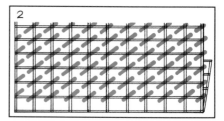

For a 9 cm (3½ in) long fringe, cut lengths of rug wool 18 cm (7 in) long. To help cut the lengths cut a long piece of card 9 cm (3½ in) wide. Wrap the wool around the card. Cut through the loops along one edge. These lengths are then hand-knotted, one at a time, through the holes in the canvas. Fold each length in half and hook through the first hole. Thread the two ends through the loop and pull tightly to form a neat knot. Work from left to right using alternate holes to form a row of tassels (diagram 3).

There are many other kinds of fringing, knots and patterns which you may like to try as shown in the

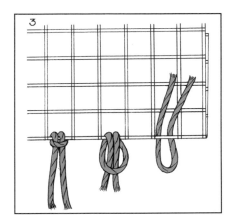

photograph. Firstly, tie together alternating tassels to make larger ones. If knotted more than once these are not only more durable, but they look tidier. Tie 1 and 3, 2 and 5, 4 and 7, 6 and 9, 8 and 11 and so on.

As a continuation, these can be knotted again, having divided the threads back to their original positions. Remember that extra yarn will be needed for the groups of knots. A series of knots on one fringe can also look attractive.

KEY to chart on pages 76-7, 80-1

☆ cream
▫ dark pink
✎ apricot
■ dark rust
✕ coral
◇ orange
▼▲ pink
✛ rust
● drab green
✱ bright green
▢ dark green

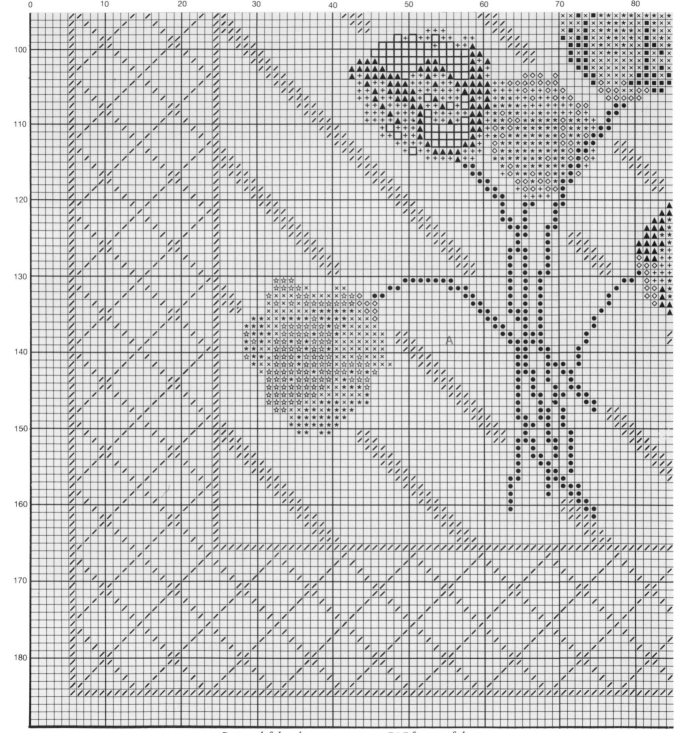

Bottom left hand quarter, see pages 76-7 for top of chart

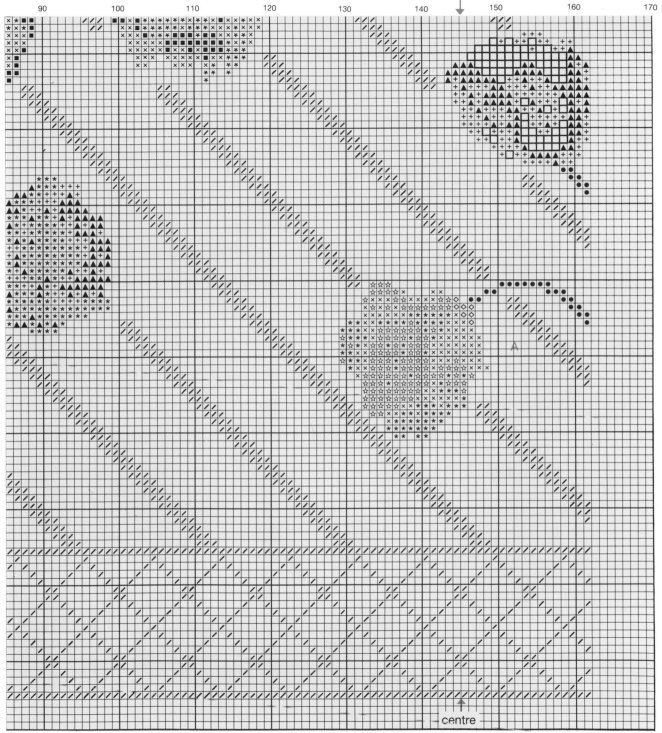

Bottom right hand quarter, see pages 76-7 for top of chart

TRELLIS FIRESCREEN

Create an attractive firescreen to cover the fireplace during the warm summer days. Embroider shaded vine leaves and grapes across a trellis framework.

This delightful firescreen makes good use of crewel wools by intermixing and blending the yarns together to produce delicately-shaded grapes and leaves. In the same way the background has several pale hues stitched in with the off-white. The trellis that criss-crosses the background uses three shades to produce an inter-woven effect. The stitching is mostly in continental tent stitch, which is ideal for working the numerous curved lines and shapes. The trellis is worked in a combination of basketweave and backstitch. The 12 hole canvas is totally covered by three strands of crewel wool.

If you have a different sized firescreen the trellis area can be extended or reduced to fit.

REQUIREMENTS					
1 piece of white interlock canvas with 12 holes to 2.5 cm (1 in), 63.5 × 58.5 cm (25 × 23 in)	*Colour*	*Appletons*	*Paterna*	Wine red (× 2)	714	911
	Pastel shades	884	314	Wine red (× 2)	716	910
	Mauve	602	324	Mauve (× 2)	604	312
	Drab green	331	644	Mauve (× 2)	606	310
Tapestry needle size 20	Grey/green	356	601	Mid blue (1	151	203
Masking tape	Dull mauve	934	D115	hank + 1		
Frame	Dull rose pink	149	900	skein)		
1 piece of lightweight polyester wadding 53 × 48 cm (21 × 19 in)	Early English green	541	644	Mid blue (1 hank + 2	153	289
	Peacock blue (× 2)	641	523	skeins)		
Firescreen, with inside measurement 51 × 46 cm (20 × 18 in)	Peacock blue (× 2)	643	602	Mid blue (1 hank)	155	533
Crewel wool as follows:	Peacock blue (× 2)	645	662	White (4½ hanks)	991	261
	Dark peacock blue (× 2)	835	660			
	Wine red (× 2)	711	914	**Finished size** 53 × 48 cm (21 × 19 in)		

PREPARATION

Bind over the raw edges of canvas and mark the centre as described in the Skill File (page 16). As this is a large project, draw in the grid lines in both directions, every 10 lines. These lines should match with the lines on the chart.

Separate the yarns into groups for trellis, leaves, grapes and background as follows:

Trellis – 151 (203), 153 (389), 155 (533)
Leaves – 835 (660), 641 (523), 643 (602), 645 (662)
Grapes – 331 (644), 356 (601), 541 (644), 934 (115), 149 (900), 711 (914), 604 (312), 606 (310), 714 (911), 716 (910)
Background – 991 (453), 884 (314), 602 (324), 151 (203), 641 (523)

STITCHING

Start with the leaves or grapes, working from the top downwards using the grid lines to check that the stitching is in the correct position (see chart on pages 86–7 and 88–9).

Next stitch the trellis outline, then the trellis lines using the chart on page 90 for the top left hand quarter. Take care to interweave the threads on the wrong side of the previously stitched lines.

Finally fill the background using either 3 strands of 991 (261) or a mixture of 2 strands of 991 (261) and 1 strand of either 884 (314), 602 (324) or 151 (203). An example of

the random shading has been charted on page 91; simply add as much or as little of the mixed strands as preferred.

Stitching the background last will help to keep the light-coloured threads clean. It is a good idea when mixing crewel threads to separate them all first before regrouping this will help the threads to lie together.

Take extra care on large areas of tent stitch, such as the background, as this stitch is one of the most difficult to obtain an even tension. In addition to the stitching guidelines as described in the Skill File (page 17), to gain a smooth finish on this firescreen, never finish and re-start a new piece of thread halfway across a line as the old piece will have become slightly thinner as you work. Remember not to leave the work in the middle of a row for a long period, such as overnight, and check the yarn before you begin to avoid any that looks slightly thicker or thinner.

MAKING UP AND FINISHING

Remove the canvas from the frame and stretch if necessary as described in the Skill File (page 73). Trim the canvas to within 2 cm (¾ in) of the stitching. Tack a piece of wadding to the wrong side at the edges. Place over the inside panel of the firescreen and pin along the edges, stretching the canvas firmly. Secure on the wrong side with masking tape, then remove the pins and fix into the firescreen.

EXPERIMENTING

This is a project where the background could be stitched in space-dyed yarns, which have very gradual colour change as described below. Apart from cold water dyes, fabric paints or spray paints can be used to tint the yarns.

For a further experiment, the leaves and grapes are ideal for stencilling. Use the outline of the stencil shown opposite to cut your own. Copy the design (enlarging it if required) onto stencil card. Using a sharp craft knife cut out the stencil. Hold the stencil temporarily on the canvas with spray adhesive, then either spray paint or sponge with fabric paints all over the canvas. Remove the stencil and when the painted canvas is completely dry, the stencilled areas can be stitched.

Space Dyeing
This type of dyeing produces a range of variegated yarns quickly and easily, although a little practice may be needed to achieve an exact result.

As dyes react differently on certain fibres, keep a record of which dyes you use, so you can reproduce similar effects. Use cold-water fabric dyes and make up as follows: mix between a quarter to one teaspoon of dye powder, this will depend on the intensity of the colour, in an old jam jar with a small amount of cold water. Add hot water to dissolve the dye. Make up a salt solution by dissolving

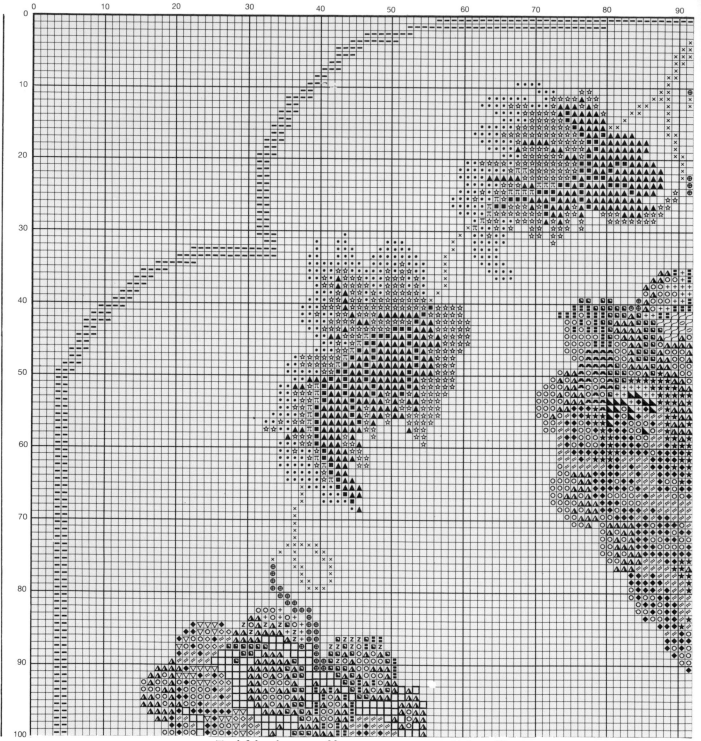

Top left hand quarter of firescreen centre, see page 90 for trellis

Bottom left hand quarter of firescreen centre, see pages 86-7 for top of chart

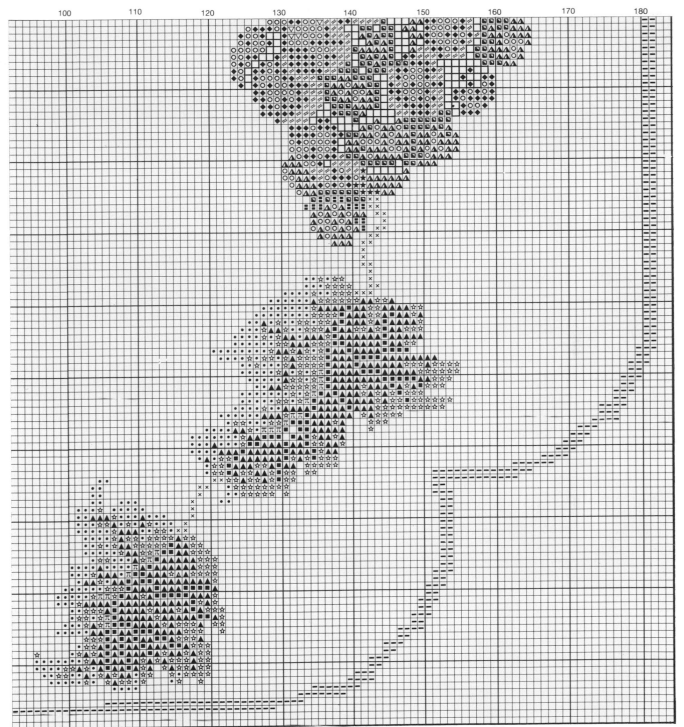

Bottom right hand quarter of firescreen centre, see pages 86-7 for top of chart

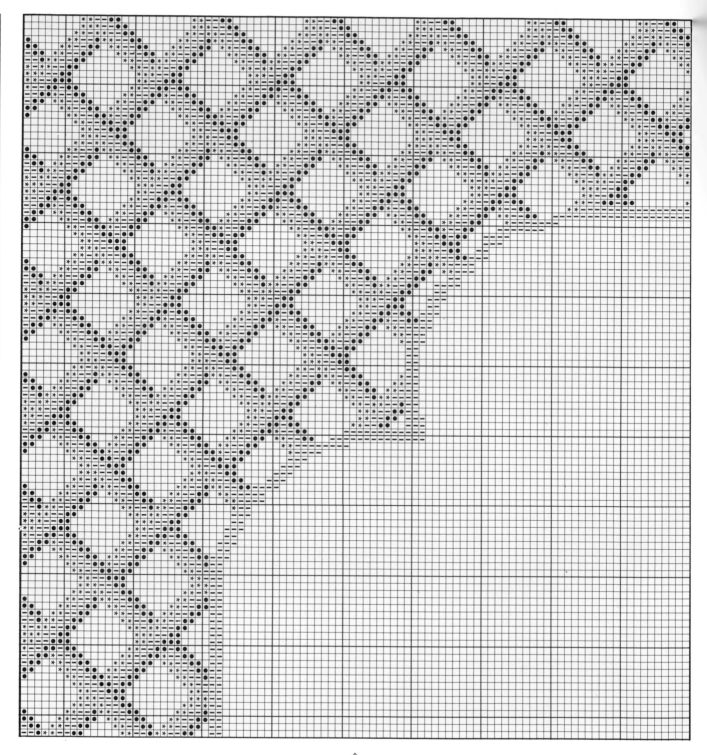

100 g (4 oz) of salt in 600 ml (1 pt) of hot water. Fill up the jam jar with the salt solution. Make up a jam jar for each dye. Tie the yarns loosely together and place in a shallow dish or tray. Spoon over the dyes using several colours in one area, making sure that there is some intermixing. Leave for 5 to 10 minutes for the dyes to penetrate.

Make up a mixture of 100 g (4 oz) of washing soda dissolved in 600 ml (1 pt) of hot water and pour over the threads. Leave for approximately 5 minutes to fix the dyes, then wash gently in mild soapy water and rinse.

The yarns can also be knotted tightly in several places and immersed in the dyes. The knots will prevent the dye from penetrating, so that areas of the original yarn colour will be left showing.

Once the threads are dry, wind them up ready for stitching. A sample of the effect is shown in the photograph below.

KEY
background shading
✎ white 991
● 991 (2 strands) + 884 (1)
× 991 (2 strands) + 602 (1)
★ 991 (2 strands) + 151 (1)

KEY to charts on
pages 86-7, 88-9, 90
grapes
O wine red 711
▲ wine red 714
◗ wine red 716
◞ 331 (2 strands) + 714 (1)
◔ 331 (1 strand) + 356 (2)
+ 331 (1 strand) + 714 (2)
⌀ mauve 606
▢ mauve 604
◤ 604 (1 strand) + 714 (2)
★ dull mauve 934
◤ 714 (2 strands) + 711 (1)
▽ 604 (2 strands) + 331 (1)
▤ dull rose pink 149
Z 716 (2 strands) + 356 (1)
℧ 604 (1 strand) + 356 (1) + 331 (1)
◇ 606 (2 strands) + 356 (1)

leaves and stalks
● peacock blue 641
☆ peacock blue 643
π peacock blue 645
▲ dark peacock blue 835
■ drab green 331
× 541 (2 strands) + 641 (1)
⊕ 541 (2 strands) + 331 (1)

trellis
★ mid blue 151
━ mid blue 153
● mid blue 155

CARE AND CONSERVATION

When the needlepoint is completed, it is a good idea to spray it with a waterproof spray, this will prevent the penetration of any spills or liquids, as well as protecting it from dirt and dust.

Regularly vacuum needlepoint articles especially rugs, upholstery and cushions, to remove the dust. This will prolong their life, since dust will eventually rot the fibres.

If necessary canvaswork objects can be dry cleaned. When the item is static an upholstery cleaner can be used instead. Dry cleaning is better than washing as shrinkage can occur and this in unequal proportions across the piece because of the different yarns and materials.

If you must wash the needlepoint, try to test the yarns first for colour fastness and only wash in warm water with a mild soap.

Avoid squeezing or wringing, rinse thoroughly and dry away from direct heat. Re-blocking will probably be necessary.

Pictures and firescreens can be covered with glass to prolong their life, but this will obscure a clear view of the stitching as well as hiding the textural quality.

Avoid placing needlepoint in direct sunlight for prolonged periods, as this will fade the colours, particularly the darker ones, as well as rotting the yarns and canvas. A strong and prolonged heat source will have a similar effect.

GLOSSARY

Chintz fabric A finely woven cotton fabric given a permanent resin finish to produce a shiny surface on one side.

Curved needles Semi-circular needles used regularly in upholstery; the smallest for fine hand sewing with button or carpet thread.

Gimp pins Coloured tacks 13 mm (1 in) long with small heads, used to attach trimmings in upholstery.

Gros point Stitching over pairs of threads on Penelope canvas.

Interlock canvas A canvas in which the warp and weft threads pass through each other rather than above or below.

Mounting board A 3 mm (⅛ in) thick, strong card available in various colours.

Penelope canvas A double thread canvas used where a combination of *petit point* and *gros point* is stitched.

Permanent marking pen A waterproof pen used to draw on designs or mark the canvas before stitching.

Petit point Stitching over single threads on Penelope canvas.

Piping cord A cord available in varying thicknesses used to emphasize, strengthen or decorate a seam line.

Ply The number of strands that wool/thread can be easily split into.

Scroll gimp A narrow trimming used in upholstery to cover raw edges and tack heads. It has a woven 'S' shape which makes it lie smoothly around curves.

Single/mono canvas An even-weave fabric in which the warp and weft threads weave over and under each other at regular intervals.

Strand The smallest single divisible unit that makes up any thread/wool.

Wadding/Batting A polyester padding available in varying thicknesses.

ACKNOWLEDGEMENTS

The author and publisher would like to thank the following company for its help in providing the firescreen and footstool for use in the photography:

MacGregor Designs, P O Box 129, Burton-on-Trent, DE14 3XH

Photographs: p.10: The Bridgeman Art Library/Victoria & Albert Museum; p.13: The Bridgeman Art Library/Bonhams

INDEX